GHOSTS
AND
EARTH
BOUND
SPIRITS

GHOSTS
AND
EARTH
BOUND
SPIRITS

Linda Williamson

piatkus

PIATKUS

First published in Great Britain in 2006 by Piatkus Books Ltd
This paperback edition published in 2010 by Piatkus

A CIP catalogue record for this book
is available from the British Library.

ISBN 978-0-7499-4030-0

The author would like to thank the following publishers for permission to quote from
their books:
John Blake Publishing (Metro) – *After-Death Communication* by
Emma Heathcote-James
College of Psychic Studies – *Light*, Vol. 107 No. 2, Summer 1987
Colin Smythe – *What Happens When You Die* by Robert Crookall
Psychic Book Club – *Philip in Two Worlds* by Alice Gilbert
Cathy Tostenson – *The Wheel of Eternity* by Helen Greaves

Edited by Steve Gove
Text design by Briony Chappell
Set in Sabon by Action Publishing Technology Ltd, Gloucester

An Hachette UK Company
www.hachette.co.uk

www.piatkus.co.uk

Contents

Acknowledgements

I would like to thank all the people who have helped me in the preparation of this book and have shared their experiences with me. Special thanks go to: Guy Lyon Playfair, Archibald Lawrie, Michael Evans, Philip Steff, Leslie Moul, Christine Holohan, Ian and Sharon Bradley, Lesley Garton, Veronica Ford-Keen, and Ann Elton. Finally, I would like to add a word of thanks to the late Eddie Burks, from whom I learned so much about earthbound spirits and how to release them.

Note: Fictitious names have been used throughout this book to protect the privacy of those concerned.

Introduction

The phone rang late one Sunday evening.

'I understand you're a medium?' a woman's voice said.

'That's right.'

'Well, I've got a ghost in my house and I'd like you to get rid of it.' She said it in a matter-of-fact way, like calling out a plumber to fix a leaky tap.

'What has been happening?' I asked.

'I don't quite know how to describe it. I haven't actually seen anything. It's just a feeling, as if I'm being watched all the time. It's creepy. And there are odd smells and noises ... could you come and have a look?'

As she lived nearby I agreed to call the following day. It turned out that the house was in a Victorian terrace, in a long street of similar properties. I rang the bell. Marjorie, as I shall call her, opened the door. She was a stout, middle-aged, no-nonsense sort of woman who looked as if she would be a match for any ghost. She ushered me into a neat but plainly furnished living room. Although her manner was polite, it was obvious that she felt uncomfortable with me.

'I've never had anything to do with mediums and the like before,' she confessed, a little sniffily. 'And I don't really believe in ghosts.' (It amuses me when people tell me they don't believe in ghosts – while at the same time claiming that their house is haunted!) 'But there's definitely something spooky going on here.'

I asked a few questions and found out that she had moved into the house a few months before. Nothing happened for a while, then she started to experience an uneasy sensation, as if someone was standing behind her. She had heard footsteps on the stairs and smelt cigarettes, although she didn't smoke. She tried to ignore these incidents but when the television changed channels by itself, that was the last straw.

'I suppose you think I'm going mad?' she asked.

'Not at all.' I reassured her that the experiences she was having were very common.

'What is it, then? Is it an evil spirit?'

I told her not to be afraid. I couldn't detect anything evil, only a poor, lost soul in need of help. My impression was that it was an old man who had lived in the house in Victorian times. I explained this to her and added, 'Could you give me a few minutes? I'd like to sit in here by myself and talk to him.'

She looked puzzled. 'Talk to him? Haven't you brought any equipment?'

It was my turn to be puzzled. 'What do you mean, "equipment"?'

'Well, I don't know – instruments to detect ghosts?'

She had obviously been watching *Ghostbusters*! I told her I didn't need anything of the kind. I didn't even use holy water or a crucifix. I wasn't going to carry out an exorcism. I was just going to help the spirit on its way.

'Is that all?' She looked at me anxiously as she left the room. 'Are you sure you'll be all right?'

'Of course. Your ghost isn't going to hurt me.'

Left alone, I closed my eyes, said a prayer and asked my spirit helpers, whom I call my guides, to come to my aid. I then focused my attention on the spirit. Although I couldn't actually see him, I sensed him as being old and frail and leaning on a stick. Sadness emanated from him. The guides told me that he had lived there for many years and that, when he died, he had remained there simply because he didn't know where else to go.

I spoke to him, sending him love and compassion. I didn't receive a response in words but I sensed that he picked up my thoughts. After a few minutes, a change came over him. The sadness lifted, replaced by a great surge of joy and relief. I knew that the guides had taken charge of him. They were leading him away into the light, that is to say, they were lifting him out of the darkness of his earthbound state and taking him to the spirit world where he would be reunited with those he loved.

I called Marjorie back in. 'It's all done,' I told her. 'He's gone.'

'Is that it, then?' She was sceptical. 'As easy as that?'

'Yes, as easy as that.' Most spirits are released with no trouble because they are glad to go.

She peered nervously round the room, then went very quiet for a moment, sensing the atmosphere. 'I must admit, it does feel different in here – lighter.'

'You won't have any more problems,' I assured her. And I explained what had happened.

She listened, but she obviously thought it was rather weird. 'Well, I'm very grateful, but ...'

'Yes?'

'I rather wish now that I hadn't asked you to get rid of him. It was exciting, having a ghost. I'm going to miss him.'

Ghosts and earthbound spirits

I left, reflecting that there's no pleasing some people. But I was glad that another soul had been released into the light. I come across cases like this all the time. People frequently appeal to me for help in getting rid of ghosts from their property. Ghosts are not confined to old buildings. They are found in modern houses as often as in ancient castles and stately homes. And if you should happen to see one, they are just as likely to be wearing jeans and a T-shirt as a long white shroud!

Most people use the word 'ghost' to describe any type of spirit being, but to me there is a distinct difference between ghosts and earthbound spirits. I will have more to say about this in a later chapter, but for now, let me explain briefly what that difference is.

A ghost is not really a person. It is a psychic imprint left behind in a particular place by someone who lived there, or perhaps died traumatically there. Their spirit, their real essence, has passed on to a higher dimension. An earthbound spirit, on the other hand, is a real person. It is a deceased man or woman who has not moved on after death as they should have done, but has become stuck in the physical environment. Earthbound spirits still retain the same personalities they had when alive and they still feel human emotions such as pain, anger and frustration, which is why I believe it is so important to help them.

When people say they have a ghost, what they usually have is an earthbound spirit. And these spirits can be assisted to move on to where they should have gone immediately after death. So why are they in this condition?

Why some spirits become earthbound

Death is no more than a transition from this world to a higher dimension. My work as a medium is dedicated to proving this and to demonstrating that those who have died can come back and communicate with those on earth. In the majority of cases, the passing is smooth and effortless. The dying person rises out of the physical body and is met by loved ones who take them to the spirit world, which is a place of light. But a small percentage of those who die do not make this transition successfully. They remain behind, lost in darkness, in a sort of limbo. They are earthbound – trapped and tied to the physical world.

There are various reasons why this can happen. Often, it is the result of a violent death. In some cases, it is because they were so attached to their home and possessions that they are unwilling to leave them. Some spirits may get stuck because of guilt or unfinished business. All these reasons, and many others, I will be examining in detail later on.

Earthbound spirits are in a confused mental state. Some of them do not even realise that they are physically dead. Because of this, they cannot help themselves. They need the help of a medium to release them. This is called spirit release or rescue work. I am not a ghostbuster – a term I detest – neither am I an exorcist. My intention is not to drive the spirits away but to assist them gently to move forward into the light.

What this book is about

In this book I am going to give you an insight into the work I do. I will explain how I release earthbound spirits, with the aid of my guides, and I will paint a picture of what it is like to be an earthbound spirit, trapped in that strange, shadowy region between the worlds.

It may be that you have picked up this book because you have experienced psychic disturbances in your house and you are wondering whether it is haunted. This is not always the case. There are other factors that can make a house feel odd or uncomfortable. I will show you how to recognise the signs of a genuine haunting, and tell you how to deal with it, either using the techniques I have provided or by finding a medium to do it for you.

Not all earthbound spirits are attached to places or houses. Some are attached to people. Occasionally, a spirit becomes earthbound because they care so deeply for someone they have left behind that they cannot leave that person's side. Their love and concern then becomes a tie that binds them to the material plane and prevents them from moving on. If you have lost someone dear to you and you sense that they are still very close, you may fear that they have become earthbound. This is generally not the case: they will have made the transition to the spirit world quite happily but will be choosing to come back and spend time with you. I will explain how you can discover if the spirit does need help and, if so, how you can set them free.

What about evil spirits? These do exist, and I have come across a few, but you will be relieved to learn that they are very rare. Even so-called poltergeists, destructive spirits who terrify people by making a noise and moving furniture around, often turn out not to be evil but just lost and frustrated. Nevertheless, even apparently harmless earthbound spirits can have a detrimental effect upon the living. Sensitive people, particularly, can absorb the spirit's feelings of depression, fear or anxiety. I have included a chapter on psychic protection, to show you how to safeguard yourself against these influences.

And finally, for the benefit of anyone who thinks they might like to undertake spirit release, I have given information about how to train for this difficult, demanding but infinitely rewarding work.

First of all, though, I want to tell you how I started on this pathway. It all began when I was a child, growing up in a house where things really did go bump in the night.

GHOSTS
AND
EARTH
BOUND
SPIRITS

1
My Story

We all knew that the house was haunted, but my parents, being of a sceptical disposition, chose to ignore it. The whole place had a depressing, heavy atmosphere. Strange bangs and thumps were heard in the night. Footsteps came from empty rooms.

One evening my mother opened my bedroom door and there in the dim light, standing by the bed, was a little lady in a long black dress. My mother let out a scream. The ghost turned ...

Actually, it was me. At that time (I was about 18) I was into Victorian costume and I had purchased the dress from an antique shop. I was just trying it on when she came in. I apologised for giving her such a fright but it was a long time before she forgave me. I suspect that the reason why she was so alarmed was that I really did look like the resident ghost, whom she had seen – though she was very reluctant to admit it.

I had been aware of the ghost for years. I called her my 'grey lady' because she was a misty grey figure. In fact, I didn't usually see her – it was more that I sensed her as an image in my mind. But a couple of times she did appear to me quite clearly, looking absolutely real and solid, an elderly woman dressed in black with a lace cap on her head. Then she disappeared or walked through a wall. I just accepted her as part of my life – but then, I suppose I've always been used to having spirits around me.

We had moved into the house when I was three. The family at that time consisted of myself, my parents, my unmarried Uncle Harry and my grandmother. Looking back, it was one of the most haunted houses I have ever come across. If I had been inclined to be nervous of the supernatural I don't suppose I would have survived childhood without becoming a nervous wreck. The disturbances were there from the beginning. My parents were woken in the night many times by what sounded like breaking glass. When they went downstairs to investigate, afraid that burglars had broken in, there was never any sign of damage, but the dog would be cowering, terrified, in a corner.

I didn't take much notice of these happenings when I was very young, but as I grew older and my psychic awareness developed I became acutely sensitive to the atmosphere of the house. There were certain rooms, especially the attic, where I didn't like to be alone. I didn't say anything about this to anyone, partly because I couldn't put my impressions into words and partly because I didn't want to be accused of imagining things.

My grandmother died when I was seven. My mother tried to explain to me that she had gone to be with Jesus but to me she was still very much there in the house. She remained close to me as I was growing up. Though I couldn't see her I could sense her presence clearly, but this didn't bother me.

In fact, it was a comfort. Young though I was, I could detect that there was a distinct difference between her and the ghost. My grandmother felt warm and loving, as she had been when she was alive. I could feel her smiling at me. Sometimes she spoke to me and I heard the words, not externally but in my mind. By contrast, the grey lady seemed distant, preoccupied, as though she was shut in her own mental world, unaware of what was happening around her.

The grey lady wasn't the only ghost. In fact, I often had the impression that the house was full of them. There was a tall, slim man I glimpsed once or twice wearing a Victorian-style suit with a wing collar. He seemed to be from the same period as the lady and I wondered whether they were connected. Both of them seemed sad and lonely. I felt sorry for them.

Then there were the nasty ghosts, as I called them. I never saw them at all, which was perhaps just as well. But somehow I seemed to know that they, and not the Victorian man and woman, were responsible for the noises and the menacing atmosphere I sensed in some of the rooms. What was really behind it I never discovered, but instinct told me that something deeply unpleasant had once happened there, something that still lingered. Perhaps it was a good thing that I was too young, and had too little knowledge of the next world, to probe and try to get to the bottom of it. If a body had been discovered buried in the cellar I wouldn't have been surprised.

As time went on I became more and more conscious of the Victorian ghosts. Whenever I felt them in the room I tried to speak to them. While there was never any response from the old woman, I felt that I made some mental contact with the man. I couldn't communicate with him in words but I sensed that he was grateful for my kind thoughts. Unlike the woman, he seemed to be aware of the present day. Once, when I was in the kitchen doing the washing, I caught a glimpse of him looking puzzled at the washing machine, as if wondering what this new-fangled contraption was. One Christmas, when I felt him very strongly present, I sent out a thought asking him to give me a sign that he could hear me. The paper chains hanging over the fireplace immediately began to rustle, although there was no draught.

The ouija board

As I have said, the Victorian ghosts never frightened me. I just wished that I could do something to help them. There was only one occasion in the house when I was really frightened – and it was my own fault.

I was about 15 years old. One of my friends at school had brought in a ouija board and we had been playing with it in the lunch hour. I found it worked quite well when I was there and we received a number of accurate 'messages', so I thought I would try by myself at home.

I sat in my bedroom late one night after everyone else had gone to bed. I had made an improvised ouija board by drawing a large circle of letters on a sheet of cardboard. I took a wine glass, turned it upside down and placed it on the board, resting my fingers lightly on top of it. Then I asked, in the time-honoured way, 'Is there anybody there?'

Slowly, the glass began to move. It seemed to have a will of its own. I felt sure that I wasn't pushing it. It spelt out the letters A N N. I was thrilled. Annie was my grandmother's name.

'Is that you, Nan?' I asked.

The glass started to move more rapidly but it was just a jumble of letters that made no sense. There was a sensation of power building up in the room, but it wasn't a good feeling. I felt as if something was trying to take me over and I knew it couldn't be my nan. She would never do anything to frighten me. The glass whizzed round faster and faster. Suddenly it spun off the table and hit the chair leg with such force that it shattered into fragments on the floor.

I was terrified. My heart was thumping. The room had gone icy cold. How I was going to explain the broken glass was the least of my problems. Whatever was in there with me definitely did not mean well. I prayed as I had never prayed before, asking for protection and repeating the Lord's Prayer over and over.

Gradually the power subsided and the room came back to normal. I breathed a sigh of relief. I went to bed, but I didn't sleep a wink that night. I didn't know then how dangerous ouija boards can be. Mischievous or malevolent spirits can use them as a way of getting through and some-times they take on false identities, pretending to be someone the user of the board loves and trusts. I resolved never to touch an ouija board again. And I never again went to sleep without saying my prayers.

Becoming a medium

Although my family was not religious, I had always instinc-tively known that there was a life after death. It seemed perfectly natural to me that, after she died, my grand-mother should still be around. When I was in my teens my awareness of the invisible world became stronger. I never felt alone. Apart from occasional glimpses of the ghosts I still didn't see anyone. It was just a sensing, a knowing that I wasn't alone. Often I heard voices in my mind. However, as my family wouldn't have understood I couldn't share this with them, and so I had no one to talk to about it.

At one point I began to doubt my voices and wondered if they were just my imagination. But then they started to tell me things that I couldn't have known about, predicting things that were going to happen. They were only trivial predictions but they convinced me that it wasn't all in my mind. I had to find out what was going on, so I went to the library and read all the books on the supernatural I could find. That was how I came across Spiritualism, and how I realised that I was a natural born medium. Unknown to anyone, I began occasionally attending Spiritualist churches. But that was as far as my involvement went until I was in my early twenties, when I married and moved away from home.

I then joined the local Spiritualist church and became an enthusiastic member. I was delighted to have the company of others who understood me and didn't think I was mad for talking to dead people. They also helped me to under-stand about ghosts, explaining how they can remain stuck for years in the houses where they used to live. I thought what an unhappy existence it must be!

My husband and I were living in the north of England at that time but we often went back to London to stay with my parents. And whenever I was there, I attuned to my guides, whom I was just getting to know, and asked them to take the poor earthbound spirits into the light. It seemed to work, because over the years I felt their presence less and I hoped and prayed that they had been released and had found their way to a happier place.

The house in which I lived with my husband was not haunted at all, although it was a Victorian building. It was quite a change for me not to sense some unseen presence every time I walked into a room. The only ghost we had was a cat. I saw it many times; sometimes it was so clear that I would bend down to stroke it – and find myself stroking empty air. My own two cats saw it as well. Often they would stand staring into space, hissing, their fur bristling, the way cats do when confronted with an intruder.

It was while we were living in the north that my father died. As with my grandmother, I felt that he was still close to me. But, because he had been so dear to me, it was vitally important to me to be absolutely sure that he really was there and that I wasn't imagining it because I wanted it to be true. I sought proof through Spiritualism, and found it in a wonderful way. I received many communications from my father: in the most remarkable, a medium described him to me, gave me his name and repeated to me the last words he said to me as he lay dying. This was when I resolved to develop my gifts and work as a medium, so that I could bring to other people the comfort I myself had received.

After a couple of years we moved back to London, where I again joined the local Spiritualist church. I began to develop my gift by sitting in what is called a development circle, a group where mediums are trained. After a while, when I felt sufficiently confident, I starting taking services in Spiritualist churches and giving private consultations – readings or sittings as they are called – in my home.

I have explained in my previous books, *Contacting the Spirit World* and *Finding the Spirit Within*, how the spirits communicate with me. Briefly, it works by a sort of telepathy. I have to attune my mind to those who wish to come through, to get on to their wavelength. They have to do the same from their side, so that a mental link is established. I home in on this link, using all my psychic awareness to pick up impressions as clearly as I can of who the spirits are, what they look like and what they want to say. I have a room in my house set aside where I do sittings and I regard this room as my sanctuary. I often sit there quietly by myself to pray and meditate.

The spirits who come through in sittings are nearly always relatives or friends of the sitters. Occasionally, though, there may be someone who died before the sitter was born but who is still interested in their earthly family. It is love that brings these people back; the next world is very close to this one, and those we care about are only a thought away. From time to time I am aware of earthbound spirits who accompany the sitters. Usually they are relatives who, for one reason or another, have not moved on, and these spirits I try to help.

Giving sittings at home forms the major part of my work. Clients come to me for a variety of reasons. Obviously, many of them come because someone has died and they are seeking proof, as I did with my father, that the person has survived death and is well and happy in the spirit world. Others are looking for spiritual guidance or want to know about the guides who are with them. Some come because they have a problem for which they need guidance. The spirits do not solve our problems for us but they can often offer valuable insights and advice.

Starting spirit release work

When I first started working as a medium I didn't know much about spirit release or rescue work. I had heard of it but I didn't feel it was something I would ever do. However, sitters would talk to me from time to time about ghosts and psychic phenomena, or say that they felt there was a spirit around them who was troubled and in need of help.

One day a medium who had a lot of experience in releasing spirits invited me to go with her to a house where the ghost of an old man had been seen. I watched what she did, noting how she spoke gently to the spirit, urging him to go into the light. It was all done very simply and lovingly. I sensed the spirit's loneliness and unhappiness and felt his joy as he was led away. And I felt a strong urge within myself to undertake this work and help others like him.

The guides must have picked up my thoughts. As if on cue, people started coming to me, asking me to investigate supernatural happenings within their homes. I was surprised to discover how common hauntings are and that there are a great many earthbound spirits around. I found that the vast majority of them were harmless and had no wish to frighten or disturb anyone. But they were suffering, and because of that, my heart went out to them, as it did to the people whose houses they were haunting: they were sometimes very frightened, not knowing what was happening or where to turn for help.

In this way I was drawn into rescue work. I realised that for me, as for many mediums who do such work, I had a double mission, both to those in this world who were experiencing problems and also to the lost and bewildered spirits.

That was the beginning of a new stage in my journey. It very quickly became clear to me how complex the subject of spirit release is and how much I had to learn. There was no one simple explanation to account for all the phenomena and no one way of dealing with it. Twenty years later, I am still learning and I don't claim to have all the answers. But I want to share with you the experiences I have had and the conclusions I have reached. And first I want to say a bit more about ghosts – and how they differ from earthbound spirits.

2
Ghosts and Earthbound Spirits

As I have said, most people use the word 'ghost' to describe all spirit beings. Mediums talk about both 'ghosts' and 'spirits', but they don't all use those words in quite the same way. When giving sittings, a medium will always refer to 'spirits' coming back to communicate. However, some mediums call spirits who haunt houses 'ghosts' while others call them 'earthbound spirits'. If all this sounds confusing – that's because it is! I have spoken to many mediums and have concluded that there is no clear definition upon which they all agree. I have therefore decided upon my own definition, which is the one I set out in the introduction to this book.

Let me remind you of that definition. Ghosts are the psychic imprints of people who once lived or died in a particular place. Earthbound spirits, on the other hand, are deceased men and women with human feelings. But sometimes it can be hard to tell which is which.

What is a ghost?

If a person has experienced intense emotion such as pain, suffering or fear in a particular place, some fragment of their energy may linger there. It can remain for many years, even for centuries, imprinted into the very bricks and stones of a building. This fragment of energy has no consciousness and cannot interact with the living. It is just the empty shell of the person, like a suit of clothing the wearer has long since discarded. The person's spirit, their real essence, has passed on into the spirit world. The fragment that is left behind is a ghost.

Ghosts are usually associated with violent or traumatic death, for the obvious reason that those who die in this way are likely to have experienced fear and suffering. Such ghosts are often wrongly assumed to be earthbound spirits.

Let us take, as an example, a house where some unfortunate man was murdered, perhaps long ago in the past. A sensitive person moves into the house. They feel the man's presence and perhaps even see him, either outwardly or with their inner vision. Not surprisingly, they conclude that the man is earthbound and haunting the house. This may be the case – but not necessarily. What the sensitive person is picking up may be just a ghost.

Any former occupant of the house who experienced intense emotion there, not necessarily because of the manner of their death but perhaps because of depression or a painful illness, might similarly leave a ghost behind. Even someone who was happy there could leave their imprint, if they had a strong personality – in which case, the house would feel as if it was haunted by a happy presence.

From my point of view as a medium, I do not perceive such ghosts as 'people'. They have a flat, one-dimensional quality. Watching one is like viewing a figure projected on to a cinema screen as opposed to watching a living person. I do not attempt to talk to them, any more than I would try to talk to a character in a film, because I know they cannot respond to me.

Ghosts can be removed, as I will describe later. But, unless they are frightening or disturbing the current inhabitants of the house, they can be left alone because they do no harm. They grow fainter and fainter over time as their energy dissipates until they fade away altogether.

Recurring apparitions

Spirits are as unpredictable in their behaviour as people. They can move around from place to place and you never know where they are going to turn up. By contrast, many ghosts behave like automatons. They always appear in the same place at the same time and go through the same actions. For this reason, they are sometimes called 'recurring apparitions'.

Perhaps the most famous example of a recurring apparition is the ghost of Anne Boleyn, Henry VIII's second wife, who was imprisoned in the Tower of London and executed in 1536 on a trumped-up charge of adultery. Ever since, so it is claimed, her ghost has been seen walking from the Queen's House where she spent her last night on earth to the place of execution, Tower Green – in the words of the old song, 'with her head tucked underneath her arm'! A fable, perhaps – but over the years more than one sentry on guard duty has heard footsteps and been approached by the headless phantom. In 1864 a sentry challenged the figure and thrust his bayonet through it, but it just carried on walking. The man fainted with shock and was brought before a court martial. But so many other sentries had reported similar encounters that he was acquitted.

I do not think it likely that the queen's spirit is forever bound to the place of her death. In all probability she has long since passed on into the light, leaving only her poor ghost to bear witness to her suffering and unjust death.

Re-enactments

Events, like people, can leave behind them a ghostly impression in the place where they occurred, not only in buildings but in the landscape. The more intense the emotions generated, the stronger the imprint and the longer it will remain. People who are sensitive to atmosphere feel uncomfortable when visiting, for example, a prison, a dungeon, a burial ground or the site of a battlefield. They may even see the events that took place there re-enacted, or hear the sounds.

A friend of mine who lived in the village of Crondall in Hampshire told me how she experienced a strange re-enactment. She was driving home late at night along a country lane when, as she described it, some invisible presence passed through her car. Looking towards the fields by the roadside, she saw what seemed to be a procession of figures in medieval dress carrying torches. The sight so unnerved her that, ever after, she drove home by a different route, even though it took her miles out of her way. Later, she learned that the field had been a burial site for victims of the Black Death, the horrific plague that swept the country in 1348.

Re-enactments have been reported from a number of battlefields. One of the best known is the site of the Battle of Gettysburg fought in the American Civil War, at which more than 50,000 men perished. Ghostly soldiers have been seen here and the noise of battle has been heard. Similar reports come from Culloden in Scotland, where in 1746 Bonnie Prince Charlie's Highlanders were defeated, with massive slaughter, by the troops of King George II.

But perhaps the most astonishing case concerns the battle of Edgehill, the first engagement of the English Civil War, fought in 1642 between Charles I and the Parliamentarians under Oliver Cromwell. Over a thousand men lost their lives in the conflict. One night soon afterwards, local people heard the sound of cannon, the beating of drums and the groans of the wounded. Then suddenly there appeared in the sky battalions of soldiers fighting out a phantom battle. The same demonstration was repeated on the following night and a crowd came to watch, some of whom recognised dead comrades among the phantoms. The performance was repeated many times, growing fainter each time. But dim echoes of the battle have been heard even in recent years.

No one really understands what causes these re-enactments. The best explanation I can give is that when someone who has psychic energy visits the site of a tragic or dramatic event, they can activate the residual energy of that event. But what they are seeing is a psychic imprint. It is as if they had pressed an invisible button and caused an old video to be replayed. The characters in re-enactments are ghosts and, like all ghosts, they eventually fade away.

Where ghosts and earthbound spirits exist together

Ghosts and earthbound spirits can, however, exist side by side in the same location. Once more, battlefields are a good example. Among the ghosts there are spirits, trapped by the trauma of their death. Should you be psychic, and should you be walking around an old battlefield – not something I recommend – you will pick up a variety of impressions and perhaps see with your psychic vision some disturbing sights. And, in the confusion, you will find it hard to tell which are ghosts and which are spirits.

The same applies when visiting any old building, such as a stately home, or an historic palace or castle. The atmosphere has been built up over the centuries, layer upon layer. Every generation has contributed, not only the aristocratic families who owned the building but the lesser members of their households, down to the humblest servant. Their joys and sorrows, hopes and fears have all been recorded on a psychic level. No sensitive person can fail to be aware of a certain 'something' in the air that sends a shiver down the spine.

It is as though the invisible residents are pursuing their own lives in a different dimension. And in a way this is exactly what is happening. Probably both ghosts and earthbound spirits are present. There may well be former occupants too, who are not earthbound but have chosen to remain in the house of which they were so proud, perhaps resenting the hordes of tourists who now traipse through their private apartments. Any medium called in to investigate such a house would need time and patience, as well as skill, to sort out one type of presence or apparition from another.

Ghosts of the road

An acquaintance once told me how she crashed her car swerving to avoid a lorry that, seconds later, simply vanished. It was a claim that failed to impress her insurance company. However, she was not alone in having an experience of this kind. There are many accounts of phantom vehicles of all types – lorries, cars and motorcycles – that appear out of nowhere and disappear just as suddenly.

Another frequently reported phenomenon is that of the phantom pedestrian who appears, usually at night on a lonely road, and steps out into the path of an oncoming car. The horrified driver slams on the brakes, convinced that a collision is inevitable. Sometimes, he feels the impact as the car runs the victim over. Yet when he gets out to look there is no one there.

A related modern phenomenon is that of the phantom hitch-hiker. In the typical version of the story, a motorist driving along a lonely road at night stops to pick up a passenger, usually a young woman, who may appear a little strange but whom he has no reason to think is not flesh and blood. At some point in the journey he looks round to find that she has disappeared. Later, he learns that a woman was killed in an accident at the place where he picked her up.

One of the most famous phantom hitch-hikers has become known as Resurrection Mary. The story goes that, in the 1930s, a young woman was at a dance with her boyfriend at the O'Henry Ballroom in the Justice district of

Illinois. They had a row and she left to walk home alone. On the way she was knocked down and killed by a car. Since then there have been numerous sightings in the area of a young woman in a white party dress. Passing motorists have stopped to pick her up and she has asked to be taken down Archer Avenue towards the Resurrection Cemetery – but when the car reaches the cemetery she vanishes.

There are many variations on this story. Some young men have claimed to have danced with a strange young woman at the ballroom. One remarked that she felt unnaturally cold. He offered to take her home in his car. She directed him down Archer Avenue towards the cemetery where she asked him to slow down. Then she darted from the car, vanishing in front of his eyes before she reached the gates.

Tales like this have become part of modern folklore. It has been suggested that the contemporary stories are modernised versions of the old tales of phantom coaches. Certainly, many of these stories sound too far-fetched to be taken seriously. Yet some, like the story of Resurrection Mary, are supported by so many witnesses that it would be rash to dismiss them out of hand. So how can they be explained?

Setting aside those that are works of fiction or hallucination, there are two possibilities. Some of these phantoms are recurring apparitions, transfixed in the spot of their death. Others, those which interact with the living, carrying on conversations with the drivers, may be earthbound spirits, trapped in the place where they died and unaware that there is anywhere else for them to go. Any motorist who has an encounter with a spirit of the road can help by sending out thoughts and prayers, asking that the spirit may be released.

Ghosts of the living

I hope I have successfully demonstrated how hard it can be to tell ghosts and spirits apart. Just to complicate matters further, I want to deal with one last category – ghosts of the living. I have said that someone who had a strong personality or who experienced intense emotion while living in a house can leave behind an imprint. But that may not necessarily be a dead person.

A client, Susan, asked me to visit her house because she felt a disturbed atmosphere in one of the bedrooms. A neighbour had told her that the previous owner of the house had a handicapped daughter who slept in that room, and Susan feared that the child's spirit might still be there.

I could sense at once that this was not the case. What had happened was that the child's feelings of unhappiness and frustration had become imprinted upon the room. For all I knew, the child was still living. All that was needed was to cleanse the room (I will explain later how this is done), after which the energy was raised and Susan was able to use it with no feelings of discomfort.

If you have a strong personality, or you suffered some trauma in a house where you once used to live, you may have left your imprint behind and the present owners may think the house is haunted!

There is a well-known story, for which I have been unable to trace the source, of a woman who had frequent vivid dreams of a house in the country. One day when she was touring a part of the country she particularly liked she saw the house, exactly as she had seen it in her dreams. She was delighted to see a 'For Sale' board outside so she knocked on the door.

The owner confessed that she was having a problem in selling the house. Prospective purchasers were put off by the fact that they sensed it was haunted.

'Who is the ghost?' the woman asked. And the startled owner of the house told her, 'It's you!' The woman had been visiting the house in her sleep state and had appeared there as a ghost.

Fact or fiction – who knows? But it's an intriguing tale!

Ghost hunting

While talking about ghosts, I feel that I must add a few words about ghost hunting. Ghosts have been studied by psychical researchers for well over a hundred years. The Ghost Club was set up in London in 1862. The Society for Psychical Research was founded in 1882, with an American branch being established a few years later. Today, ghost hunting is a popular pastime. Groups have sprung up all over the world, some more serious and better qualified than others.

Ghost hunters stake out a building, be it a house or an ancient ruin. They take with them an array of equipment, including cameras, tape recorders, thermometers, EMF detectors to register changes in the electromagnetic field, and motion detectors to pick up the slightest supernatural movement. They then sit and wait for spooky thrills. Very often, nothing happens at all. Occasionally they may be rewarded by a sudden drop in temperature or an anomalous reading on their instruments.

But these enthusiasts often refuse to involve mediums in their investigations, feeling that this is in some way 'unscientific'. They fail to distinguish between different types of spirit beings, viewing them all as 'entities' to be analysed and dissected. They do not appreciate that some of these 'entities' may be deceased people who are suffering and in need of help. To me, this is rather like going to a scene where someone is drowning and measuring the temperature of the water and testing the currents, while completely ignoring the screams of the poor victim crying out to be saved.

Nor are ghost hunters of much use when called in to a haunted house. They set up their equipment, hoping for something spectacular to happen – the scarier, the better! They want to encourage the ghost to perform. The householder doesn't want the ghost encouraged, he just wants to get rid of it. But the efforts of the ghost team can sometimes make things worse. They stir things up, leaving behind a very indignant spirit who then takes out his fury on the unfortunate inhabitants of the house!

Shutting up shop

In fairness, I should add that not all ghost hunters and psychical researchers approach the subject in such an unsympathetic way. One researcher who does have an understanding of the spirit world and who recognises the value of involving mediums to help earthbound spirits is Archibald Lawrie, secretary of the Scottish Society for Psychical Research. In his long experience he has investigated hundreds of cases and he receives several calls a week from people troubled by psychic activity in their homes or places of work. He seeks to alleviate their fear by explaining to them what is happening.

Archie told me, 'I use the help of a medium in every case. Mediums are the only way we have into this other world. It is a very successful method of research and for the most part no second visit is needed.'

In many instances he finds that very little needs to be done to help the spirit move on. Kind thoughts and gentle words are all that are required. The very fact that the spirit has made contact and has felt the compassion being directed towards it is enough to break the mental chains binding it to the earth.

In *The Psychic Investigator's Casebook* Lawrie recounts many fascinating stories of spirits he has encountered. One particularly intriguing example concerned a shop in the small Scottish town of Crighton, run by a Mr and Mrs Huttons. Every night for a number of years, goods on the shelves had been moved. Several times Mrs Huttons had seen a small, bent man in dark clothing. Perhaps strangest of all, whenever the Huttons were working in the shop late at night, at 10.30 they felt an irresistible compulsion to get out of the shop and go home. They experienced no fear, just a strong feeling that it was time to go.

Archie visited the shop with Francesca, the talented medium with whom he often works. It didn't take her long to get to the bottom of the mystery. Francesca saw the old man walk from the street to a spot halfway through the shop, then turn and walk through the shelves into a doorway that once led to a flight of stairs. As Francesca talked to the old man she was able to fit together the pieces of the story. When he had been alive the area where the shop was later built had been a covered way into the court-yard of an inn. The man had worked at the inn and his lodgings had been in the rooms above. He was responsible for seeing to the security of the inn, and every night at 10.30 he would walk through the courtyard, driving out into the street any locals who were hanging around, before shutting the doors and retiring to his rooms.

Usually mediums will encourage a trapped spirit to move on in order that it can progress. In this case, however, the spirit seemed quite content to remain there and the Huttons were not disturbed by his presence, so it was decided to let him stay.

Archie Lawrie's approach is one which I and all mediums would heartily endorse. Any earthbound spirit one encounters during an investigation should be treated with compassion and understanding. This thought is very much in my mind whenever I am called out to a haunted house.

So how are spirits released? In order to explain this, I shall next describe some of the cases I have dealt with, cases in which house owners have experienced some very strange goings-on.

3

Help – We've Got a Ghost!

Some people realise as soon as they move into a house that there is something wrong. For others, the awareness gradually dawns upon them that strange things are happening for which there is no rational explanation. It is at this point that they take fright and say, 'Help – we've got a ghost!' And that is when I get a panic-stricken phone call.

The caller is usually a woman, since women are, on the whole, more sensitive to these things than men. They are often quite embarrassed about what is going on, as though they expect me to tell them that they are imagining things. Of course, I never do that. I reassure them that they are not going mad and that what seems so strange and frightening to them is probably something I am quite familiar with.

Having calmed them down, I ask them to give me more detail about what has been happening. For instance, have they felt a presence? Or have there been inexplicable smells or noises? Such phenomena are common indications of a haunting. Or is it something more frightening, like the furniture being moved? Fortunately, spirits who do anything like this are most unusual.

I am surprised if anyone tells me they have actually seen an apparition, except perhaps as a shadow or a fleeting glimpse caught out of the corner of the eye. Much more common are feelings or sensations, such as a sense of being watched, a vague unease, or an impression that there is something odd or uncomfortable about the house, though they can't quite define what it is.

If the house is a long way from where I live I try to find a medium in the caller's area who is able to visit them. Hauntings can sometimes be dealt with at a distance but it is better if a medium can investigate in person. If the caller lives near me, I will offer to go and see them and attempt to cleanse the house of any ghosts or earthbound spirits who may be around. This is what mediums call doing a 'clearing' – and it gives a whole new meaning to the expression 'house clearance'. My offer is usually taken up with alacrity by the caller. 'Oh, yes, please come,' is the relieved reply. 'And as soon as you can!'

And so I arrange a time for a visit. In many cases, the whole family wants to be there, out of curiosity if nothing else, but sometimes the lady of the house arranges to smuggle me in at a time when her sceptical husband is out at work!

Before the day comes, I have some preparation to do. I attune to my guides and ask them to give me an indication of the kind of problem I will be dealing with. Is it really a haunting? If so, is it what I have come to regard as a typical case where a harmless spirit continues to exist in its former home? Or is it something more unusual and possibly difficult to handle? I spend some time projecting my thoughts towards the house to see what I can pick up. My guides also start work there, preparing the way for when I arrive.

Prior to leaving home on the day of my visit, I carry out my final preparation. This consists of a few minutes of prayer. I also wrap myself mentally in a psychic cloak of protection, just in case it is needed. Then I make a careful study of the map – otherwise I am bound to get lost! – and set off.

Arriving at the house

When I arrive and meet the person who contacted me, they often appear quite nervous – though sometimes they seem to be more frightened of me than they are of the ghost! They are relieved to discover that I am fairly normal. I sit them down to discuss the problems they have been experiencing. I reassure them that there is most unlikely to be anything evil involved, since evil spirits are very rarely encountered. Any phenomena produced by spirits are just their way of drawing attention to themselves. How else can they let anyone know of their existence?

I ask the client a few questions. Have they lived in the house a long time? Have the phenomena been going on since they arrived or have they just started? Have the owners recently made any changes to the property or carried out renovations? Such activity often seems to trigger off a haunting. In fact, the spirit was probably there all the time, but the alterations have disturbed it and it is showing its displeasure!

While I make these enquiries I am sensing the atmosphere of the house. A house that is haunted has a particular kind of energy about it, hard to define but instantly recognisable. It is a coldness, but it is different from physical cold. I walk around each room in turn, assessing where the atmosphere is strongest. This room is the focal point of the haunting. There may be 'cold spots', small, localised areas of concentrated energy. The householder invariably says these areas are impossible to warm up, no matter how high they turn up the heating.

By this time it will, hopefully, have become clear to me what the cause of the problem is. Although it might well be an earthbound spirit, there are a number of other possibilities.

Natural causes

This is the first and most obvious thing to consider. I have never come across a case where a client has been lying to me. I have heard of cases where tenants in a house have claimed that they had a haunting in order to persuade the council to rehouse them. And of course, children, or even adults, have been known to play tricks, either to frighten other members of the family or for sheer devilment. But all the clients who have sought my help have been genuinely concerned and worried.

Fear, however, can lead people to think there is something present when in fact there is not. Many people have a deep-rooted fear of the supernatural. It is easy for a nervous person to imagine things, particularly if they are alone in the house. Any creak, bang or rattle is attributed to a supernatural cause. On the other hand, there are people who want to believe the house is haunted because they find the idea exciting. Even when it is gently pointed out to them that the 'footsteps' they hear are only the floorboards creaking, or that a picture fell from the wall because the nail was loose rather than because it was thrown by a ghostly hand, they still refuse to accept it.

Ghosts

Ghosts are much more common than earthbound spirits. The older your house, the more likely it is that you will be sharing it with one or two ghosts. Most ghosts go unnoticed, unless their energy is particularly strong or the person who lives in the house happens to be psychic.

Some people, on first moving into a house, feel that the property is still occupied by someone who lived there before. This may be an earthbound spirit but it is just as likely to be the psychic impression of a former resident. After a time this energy generally fades, dispelled by the energy of the newcomers.

I once purchased a flat where an old woman had lived for many years. For the first few weeks I felt her presence very clearly. I decided, however, that it was just an energy trace and that her spirit had progressed to the next dimension. And this proved to be the case. Once I had redecorated the flat and stamped my own personality on it, all sense of the old woman disappeared.

If a client tells me that their spectral tenant is always seen or felt in the same place and always follows the same routine, I suspect that it may indeed be a ghost. I have to be careful, however, not to leap to conclusions. One couple reported to me that they were aware of an old man. Every night, at the same time, they heard him walking up the stairs. It turned out that this was an earthbound spirit who was simply doing what he had done every night of his life – going upstairs to bed at precisely the same time. Once he was released, the footsteps were heard no more.

Negative energy

Some clients believe that their house is haunted because it has a heavy, oppressive atmosphere. However, such an atmosphere might be due simply to negative energy. This may have been created by the previous occupants. If the house was lived in by a family where there was disharmony, anger and tension, a disturbed energy will have been left behind that can affect the newcomers.

A young couple told me that their marriage had been blissfully happy before they moved house. But since being in their new home they had done nothing but bicker, and they feared they were heading towards a divorce. I couldn't feel any spirit presence in the house, so I suggested they make discreet enquiries with the neighbours about the people from whom they had bought it. They discovered that these people had quarrelled constantly. Once the house was cleared, the couple's relationship returned to normal.

There may be a residue of negative energy from a previous building on the site. A house built on the site of, say, a hospital or a prison is not likely to be a happy place to live. The cause of the problem may be hard to establish; it may even relate to something that happened on the site before the house was built. And another factor to take into consideration is the natural energy of the land. Negative ley lines or geopathic stress can cause a depressed atmosphere. I will return to the subject of negative energy of various kinds in Chapter 6.

Tension in the family

In a few cases I have come across, the negativity was generated not by anything or anyone connected with the history of the house but by the family who called me out. On one occasion, I received a request for help from a young mother who claimed that her house was haunted by a malevolent spirit. The house was large and immaculately furnished. The woman, her partner and her three children seemed to be an ideal family. They insisted that the spirit was spoiling their lives by making them bad-tempered and irritable with each other.

I walked round the house and couldn't detect any sort of presence. But I sensed that all was not as it first appeared and that tensions were simmering under the surface. When I returned to the room where the family were sitting, there was already a heated exchange going on about who the 'spirit' might be. They were most indignant when I said that there wasn't a spirit there at all!

Situations like this are delicate. Great tact is needed to point out to the family that they are causing the bad atmosphere themselves. Some people prefer to think that they have a haunting because it gives them some external cause to blame. However, if they do acknowledge the problem honestly and take steps to resolve their difficulties, the energy of the house will improve.

Deceased relatives

One of the questions I ask clients is whether anyone in the family – not necessarily someone living in the house – has died recently. Some spirits are family members calling in to see how their relatives are. They are quite put out to be treated like troublesome ghosts!

One woman called out a medium in a panic because she had seen a 'little old lady' standing by her bed. She was terrified that it was a demon out to get her. In fact, the 'little old lady' was an aunt she had not seen for years and who had died a few weeks before. The medium spoke to the aunt, who apologised for giving her niece such a fright. All she had wanted was to say hello!

Carrying out a release

Assuming that I have eliminated all other possible causes, and that I am sure there is an earthbound spirit in the house, I then set about releasing it. Generally, there is nothing difficult involved in this and it does not take long. If the client is psychically aware I invite them to work with me. Some people are glad to do this: they are interested in what is happening and want to be part of it. Others are far too nervous: whatever I am going to do, they don't want to be there when I do it! So I suggest they go and make themselves a cup of tea, while I sit by myself for a few minutes and do my work.

I settle myself in the room where I feel the spirit's presence most strongly. Then, having first made a connection with the guides to invoke their power, I tune in to the spirit. As a rule, I don't so much see the spirit as gain a mental impression of what it looks like and a sense of its personality. I talk to it in my mind, telling it to look for a light and go towards it. I may not be able to hold a conversation with the spirit or get much of a response, as many earthbound spirits are unable to communicate clearly. However, this may not be important. All I have to do is to concentrate on sending the spirit love and compassion, and I know that the guides will be doing the same.

As I do this, the guides create a close mental link between me and the spirit. I do not go into a trance and the spirits do not take me over or possess me, but I blend my consciousness with theirs. This enables me to pick up impressions of how they died and what it is that is holding them earthbound. At this point I am aware of and able to share their emotions and, in most cases, what I sense is a deep sadness and loneliness. I often find tears pouring down my cheeks – but it is the spirit's tears I am crying.

Earthbound spirits feel lost and abandoned. In fact, they are not abandoned at all. There are other spirits present, in many cases their own loved ones, who are trying to reach them. However, the earthbound spirits are tied in their consciousness to the material world and cannot see these other spirits who are on a higher plane of consciousness. But they can see and hear the medium, because the medium is still in a physical body, and they know that, at last, someone is aware of them.

I now hold the spirit steady in the light the guides and I are projecting. This has the effect of raising its level of consciousness just sufficiently that it is able to see other spirits. It is like waking up someone who is sleep-walking.

Once this is achieved, the guides take over and lead the spirit away. I never cease to be amazed at how quickly and easily this can be accomplished. Often it takes just a few minutes. Then I feel the sadness and heaviness lift and I know that the spirit has gone.

The rescuers

I have referred many times to the guides. Every medium or healer, in fact everyone who is working spiritually, has guides who walk beside them. These are advanced beings who have chosen not to ascend further into the higher realms but to remain close to the earth plane in order to serve mankind in various ways. Some are healers, some are bringers of wisdom. Others aid communication between the worlds, enabling those who wish to contact loved ones on earth to do so. I have often been asked who my own guides are. I have a number of guides. Some are very personal to me – they have been my companions since I came into this world and they watch over me in every aspect of my life. Others come for a specific purpose.

All mediums who do rescue work have guides who are, to put it in earthly terms, specialists in such work. I call them rescuers. I have a band of rescuers around me. Whenever I go to a house where there has been a psychic disturbance, whenever I deal with someone who has an earthbound spirit attached to them, these are the helpers I call upon. They are infinitely loving, patient and strong. No spirit, however dark, is beyond their reach. I rely on them totally and without them I could do nothing. In fact, it is they who do the work. I just help out a bit!

In every case, I call upon them to guard and protect me from any negative forces I may encounter. Not that this is often needed, but I like to be on the safe side! Spirits, earthbound or otherwise, are as diverse as people on earth. Mostly they are benevolent, but I have come across some nasty characters, so I never know what may be lurking round the corner.

The students' flat

One evening I received a desperate phone call from a young man called Paul, a student at a local college. He shared his house with a number of fellow students, several of whom, he told me, had seen a ghost in the building. They had been getting more and more scared, to the point where, the night before, they had run out of the house and walked the streets, too frightened to return.

Although I agreed to Paul's request to pay them a visit, I must admit that I was nervous. I hadn't been doing rescue work long at that time and I was concerned as to whether I could handle this situation on my own, or whether I should call in a more experienced medium to help me. But my guides told me that it would be perfectly safe for me to go alone, so I set off – but not without some trepidation.

The house was in a run-down street where many of the properties had been converted into flats and let out to tenants. As soon as I stepped inside the door I felt tension in the air. There were four or five students living there, and they told me that they had all felt a presence. One of the girls had seen an evil-looking old man looming over her while she was in bed. Another had heard what she described as demonic laughter. Clearly, they had all been shaken by their experiences. But they tried to make light of it, so there was laughter as well as curiosity as I sat down with them and explained a little about ghosts and spirits.

I told them that people don't change when they die. All that happens is that they shed the material body. Those who were violent and aggressive don't become angels and sprout wings, they just become violent and aggressive spirits. They are the hooligans and yobs of the spirit world. Like characters of the same type on earth, they enjoy bullying and frightening people. Once they are dead they can't harm anyone physically but they can still behave in a menacing way, especially towards those whom they perceive to be vulnerable and easily scared. And I told the students that they were inadvertently giving power to the spirit. Fear feeds on fear and the more nervous and excited they became, the more they generated an energy which he could draw upon.

While we were talking I became aware of the man himself. He was standing in a corner of the room, listening with great interest to our conversation. He was tall and strongly built, dressed in rough clothes like a labourer. His manner was intimidating and he obviously didn't like me being there. But the only way to deal with a bully is to face up to him. So I positioned myself directly in front of him to show that I and my guides were not to be trifled with. Even as I was doing this (quaking a little inwardly, I have to admit) I sensed that, underneath his aggressive manner, he was really just as frightened as the students were. And I knew that the rescuers felt nothing but compassion for him.

Having told the students this, I went on to explain to them briefly about rescue work and suggested that we all join together in order to release him. They were open-minded enough to agree to this suggestion. So we sat round in a group. I asked them to close their eyes and I said a prayer. I then asked them to visualise the man not with fear but with pity, and to imagine him being surrounded by light. We did this for a few minutes and the room was very quiet. Then, gradually, I began to feel the atmosphere change. It was as though there were angels all around us. One of the students actually remarked that she could see a light around us all.

No words were needed. The man was shrinking before my eyes, all his bravado gone, and I caught a glimpse of the pathetic, unhappy being he really was. By now he could see the guides. At first he was afraid of them, dazzled by their brilliance and fearful, no doubt, of where they might be taking him. Spirits like this are often reluctant to leave because they think they will be taken to a place of punishment. But the guides must have reassured him that their intention was not to punish but to heal him. The rescuers never judge. They have a profound insight into what makes each spirit the way it is and what hardships or lack of love in its earthly life may have warped its character.

After a few minutes he went off with them. I explained to the group what had taken place. They were very relieved that their ordeal was over – but not half as relieved as I was, as I got into the car and drove away!

A sadness shared

Even friendly and benevolent spirits can have a damaging effect upon the people whose homes they inhabit. They may not produce psychic manifestations or do anything frightening. The damage they cause is more subtle – but it can be just as devastating.

Julie phoned me because she had been told about me by a friend. 'This probably sounds daft,' she began, 'but I think there's somebody in my bedroom.' She explained that she couldn't sleep at night because of the sensation that there was someone watching her.

I asked if she was frightened.

'No, not frightened exactly. Just uneasy. I feel it's a woman. She seems friendly and I think she likes me. But I'd like to know who she is and what she wants.'

I went to Julie's house, which from its style appeared to have been built in the 1950s. After a few minutes' discussion she showed me round. The whole house had a sense of sadness. Julie, who was in her forties, told me that she had just been through a painful divorce. As part of the settlement, the house she shared with her husband had been sold and she had moved here. At first she hadn't noticed anything strange. She thought it was a nice little house and she had hoped it would be a place where she could put the past behind her and make a fresh start.

'Then I gradually started to sense that I wasn't alone here,' she told me. 'There was a presence. I felt it in every room but particularly in the bedroom. I didn't feel it was anything bad. I just got a great sense of sadness.'

For a long time Julie put this down to her own sadness and sense of loss. The divorce hadn't been of her choosing. She still loved her husband and the separation from him felt, as she described it, like a bereavement. She knew it would take her a long time to come to terms with it. She was, in any case, quite a lonely person with few close friends and no family. But she was determined to make changes in her life. She smartened herself up, took up new interests and became involved in the community. By doing so she hoped to make friends and even possibly to meet someone to share her life with.

'But it didn't work,' she continued her story. 'In fact, as time went on I was just getting more and more depressed. I couldn't shake it off. I found I was spending more and more time in the house, just sitting and thinking.'

And she was becoming more and more strongly aware of the spirit. 'I've always been psychic and I know my grand-mother is always with me – I was very close to her. I knew she wouldn't let me come to any harm, so I meditated and tried to tune in to the woman in the house. I talk to her every day now and I believe she hears me. But I think she needs help.'

'I think you both need help,' I told her. And by now it was clear to me what was happening.

When a sensitive person lives in a house that is haunted they can unconsciously pick up whatever the spirit is feeling. Thus they may find themselves, for no apparent reason, becoming depressed, anxious, fearful, angry, or experiencing emotions which may be quite out of character and for which they can find no cause. It does not occur to them that they are being influenced by a spirit.

This was what was happening to Julie. When I linked tele-pathically with the spirit I learned that she had been a widow. Like Julie, she had lived in the house alone, grieving for her husband. She was drawn to Julie because she felt an affinity with her. In her own way she was trying to bring comfort but all she was doing was making Julie feel worse. Julie was carrying the spirit's pain as well as her own and it was such a heavy burden that she was being stifled by it.

I explained this to Julie, who was greatly relieved. 'So it's not all me!'

She asked if I could release the spirit, and this we did together. The rescuers brought the woman's husband to her. I sensed the wonderful moment of reunion when she saw him and knew that he had been waiting for a long time, unable to reach her before now.

Julie asked me whether I was aware of her grandmother.

'Your grandmother has gone into the light,' I told her. 'When she comes, she brings you light and strength. But your spirit lady, because she had got stuck, was so absorbed by her own sadness that she made you more depressed.'

The energy of the house lifted after the spirit had been released. It was like opening the curtains and letting in the sunlight. Julie missed her company at first but she was glad to know that the spirit had found happiness. With the oppressive sadness gone, she felt renewed energy to get her own life back together again, no doubt with the help of her loving grandmother. Soon afterwards she found a new partner who moved in with her. I hope her kindly spirit would have approved.

The old lady by the fireplace

It's not only clients – sometimes friends ask for my assistance if they are experiencing a problem with a haunting. My friend Ann appealed to me for help because she had become increasingly concerned about the presence of an old lady she could sense in her house. She asked me to call round and see if there was anything I could do.

Although I had known Ann for some time, I had never visited her home before. As soon as I stepped through the door I felt the familiar chill I had come to associate with haunted houses, and I knew there was someone there. The feeling was strongest in the living room and, as we sat in there with a cup of tea, Ann told me the story.

'I never really wanted this house, but we had been looking for somewhere to live for ages and this place seemed to have everything we needed. It was in the right location and there were enough bedrooms for all the boys. But I noticed as soon as we moved in that there was a terrible atmosphere. It was depressing and unfriendly. This room was particularly bad. None of us wanted to come in here. We all crowded into the kitchen! Even visitors who came to the house said there was something wrong with it. It was always cold, no matter how much we turned up the heating. I detected a cold spot over there.' She indicated the far corner of the room.

'One day I did a meditation in here. I had the impression of an old lady. I seemed to be seeing the room as it had been in her day. There was an old iron fireplace where the electric fire is and an iron bedstead in that corner. The experience was so vivid that I was shaken, so I decided to call you.'

As Ann was speaking I became aware of the old lady. I sensed that she had had trouble with her legs and that, towards the end of her life, she had been unable to get upstairs, so she had converted this room into a bedroom. She had died in here, alone.

Ann is a healer and is closely attuned to her guides, although she had never carried out a rescue. However, knowing that her positive energy would help, I suggested that we work together. We both focused our thoughts on the old lady. Without any words being spoken, I could sense what she was feeling – utterly lost, lonely and confused. We both simply sent out love to her. I projected to her the thought that we were there to help her.

For a while, nothing happened. Then, slowly, the light that was being sent to her began to penetrate her troubled mind. Now, I knew, she was seeing the guides. They were holding out their hands to her. She was unwilling at first to go with them, afraid to leave the place with which she was familiar, but they continued to coax her gently and at last she was persuaded that they had come to take her somewhere better.

Ann and I both felt her relief and it brought tears to our eyes. She was thanking us for helping her. The atmosphere of the room lightened, becoming warmer. She was ready to move on. But before she left, she told me that there would be one last manifestation of her presence.

She kept her word. A few days later, Ann went into the room. It was her son's birthday and she had put up his birthday cards on a shelf in a corner of the room where the old lady's bed had been. As she watched, all the cards fell to the floor, although there was no draught. It was the spirit's farewell. After that, Ann never felt her there again and she and her family were at last able to be comfortable in their living room.

The ghost of the workhouse

I have said that negative energy in a house may be left over from a previous building on the site. Sometimes earthbound spirits can also remain from a previous building. They are still occupying the same physical space they did in life, although of course in another dimension, and they probably don't even know that the place they inhabited isn't there any more.

Theresa was one of those people who seem to be drawn to haunted houses – this had been the case all her life. But when she moved into a newly built house on a small estate she thought that she would be free of ghostly interference. How wrong she was!

After she had been in the house for a few weeks she started picking up feelings of heaviness and fear and realised she had an invisible tenant. When I arrived at the house in answer to her request for help I sensed that the spirit was that of an elderly man, and that he was in pain. In my mind I heard him moaning, 'My legs! My legs!'

As I tuned in, I knew it was going to be difficult to reach him because he was so enclosed in his own mental world. I could not talk to him, so I never discovered whether he suffered from disease or whether his legs had been injured or amputated. All I knew was that he had died in pain and had carried that pain with him beyond the grave.

Let me hasten to explain, especially for the benefit of anyone who may have seen a loved one die in pain, that this is not the normal way of things. The spirit body, in which we exist when we shed the physical body, is perfect, without sickness or weakness of any kind. Any pain we had in life instantly disappears. In fact, those who have passed over into the spirit world say that they feel well and strong and more alive than they ever did on earth. Even earthbound spirits usually leave behind them all physical suffering. But occasionally, as in this case, their minds are so fixated on the pain they endured that they believe they are still in that condition. They do not understand that they now have a spiritual body instead of a physical one.

While I was wondering how to get through to this man, I felt one of the rescuers come forward. There was an outpouring of immense love and I heard the words, 'He has suffered enough.' That was it – he was gone.

I recounted this to Theresa and we speculated as to where the spirit might have come from, since no one had lived in the house before her. There was a hospital nearby and we wondered whether he had been a patient there. Then she told me that the house was built on the site of a Victorian workhouse. This, I felt sure, was the explanation. I could imagine the conditions of hardship and poverty in which the man must have died. No wonder the guides said he had suffered enough!

While we were talking, Theresa's eight-year-old daughter Kelly was sitting on the sofa, drawing and colouring and apparently taking no notice of our conversation. But before I left, she showed me her picture. She had written the word 'rescue' in large letters across the bottom of the page. Above it, she had drawn grey clouds and, above the clouds, a golden sun and a bright blue sky. The picture perfectly symbolised the earthbound spirit rising out of the dark clouds of unhappiness into the light above.

What is it like?

The examples I have given in this chapter are typical of the cases I come across all the time. Most people are so relieved to be rid of the haunting that they don't give much thought to the spirit or why it was there. But some people take a more sympathetic attitude. They view the spirit as I do, not as a vague, nebulous entity but as a person in need of help.

From the time when I first began releasing spirits I wondered what their existence must be like. Of course, we cannot know for sure. Earthbound spirits are individuals and vary in the way they think, feel and behave. But because of the communication I have had with them, I have gained an insight into their mental state. And this enables me to offer some answer to the question, 'What it is like to be earthbound and to dwell in that strange shadowy state between the worlds?'

4

Existence as an Earthbound Spirit

My first insight into what it is like to be an earthbound spirit occurred many years ago, not long after I had started doing spirit release work. It was, I believe, an experience given to me by my guides so that I would understand more of the state of mind of the beings I was being called upon to deal with.

I was staying with my uncle at the time. One evening I was tired and had gone to bed early, leaving him sitting in the lounge watching television. I was very concerned about him as he was seriously ill, and I lay awake for some time worrying about him before I drifted off to sleep.

Some time later I woke and decided to check that he was all right. I got up and went downstairs. As I neared the bottom of the stairs I could hear the sound of the television. The lounge door was shut. I put out my hand to open the door but somehow I found myself standing on the other side. I glanced round the room. Everything was as normal. Looking down at myself, I saw that I was wearing the same blue blouse and skirt I had been dressed in that day. My uncle had fallen asleep. I reached out and touched him – but my hand went through him.

Only at that point did it occur to me that I was having an out-of-the-body experience. I paused, wondering what to do next. Then, without consciously willing it, I found myself going back upstairs. I woke up in bed, my heart beating fast, feeling shaken and disorientated.

OBEs and earthbound existence

Out-of-the-body experiences (OBEs) are, of course, very common and have been well documented. In fact, we all have OBEs every night. Whenever we go to sleep, the spirit body detaches itself from the physical and wanders around. It can travel great distances but often it stays close to the physical. Like a ghost, it is in the same location but in a different dimension, a different state of consciousness. The reason we don't remember our nocturnal travels is because the conscious mind is dormant. Sometimes, however, the conscious mind wakes up and this is what is called an out-of-the-body experience. I have had many such experiences in my life, and I now understand how this state may resemble that of a person who passes permanently out of the body but remains earthbound.

When, in my disembodied state, I got up and went downstairs I had no sense that I was outside my body. Physically, I felt quite normal. But mentally, looking back on it, I reflected that I had felt curiously flat and unemotional. I seemed detached, as if I was watching everything from behind a sheet of glass. In the bizarre way that, in dreams, one doesn't question the odd and illogical things that happen, it never occurred to me to question the fact that I could walk through the door. Everything – the room, the furniture – looked as it always did. Yet I knew that I was helpless to move anything and that no one would know I was there. Had my uncle opened his eyes at the moment when I touched him and had he seen me, he would have thought he was seeing a ghost.

'I must be dead!'

What would have happened if, instead of being out of the body, I had died in my sleep? Then I am sure I would have been taken care of. There might have been a brief period of confusion but because of my knowledge of life after death, I would have realised very quickly what had happened. I have no doubt that my father or my grandmother would have been there to meet me. But suppose I had no knowledge of anything beyond, that I had been convinced that death is the end? Then I might indeed have been bewildered, as many people are who die suddenly and unexpectedly. I might not even understand that I had died.

That seems an extraordinary statement to make. How can you not know that you have died? But it is quite possible. When someone leaves the physical body at death they may not at first notice any change, because they are still the same person they were the moment before. They have a spirit body which looks and feels like the physical one. They are even dressed in the kind of clothes they habitually wear because the spirit self creates its clothing by an unconscious, automatic process of thought. But their mind is in a semi-conscious, dreamlike state. They are unable to think clearly, to grasp what is going on. The idea of life beyond death may be too strange for them to understand.

This state of confusion doesn't usually last long. Some spirit loved one comes to help them, gently waking them up. And at this moment – or perhaps at the moment when they look down and see their own physical body – the truth dawns: 'I must be dead!' However, there are a few unfortunate spirits who, for reasons I will come to later, do not experience this awakening. They remain in their dim, dreamlike state and this dream becomes their reality. Gradually, as time goes on – though they have no sense of time passing – they cease to be aware of the world of the living or, if they are aware of it at all, it seems like a troublesome intrusion into their dream. But, being imprisoned within their own minds, they are cut off from the spirit world as well, and the rescuers find it hard to reach them.

I said that such spirits do not know that they are dead but I suspect that, in most cases, this is not quite true. They do know, on some level, but they refuse to acknowledge it. They are afraid to move away from the place that is safe and familiar. The old lady haunting Ann's house was in this condition. What was her existence like? I cannot, of course, give a complete answer to that question but I can speculate, based on what I picked up from her and what I have gathered from other earthbound spirits. So, in order to give some idea, I will tell her story, as I have imagined it. I never discovered her name, so I will call her Alice.

Alice's story

Alice, let us suppose, had lived alone in the house for many years. She had few friends and she seldom went out, particularly in her latter years when she found it hard to walk. Like most people of her generation, she was probably brought up to believe that, when you died, you went either to heaven or hell. Perhaps she believed that, perhaps not. Maybe she never even thought about life after death.

One night she fell asleep, as she believed, and woke next morning feeling still herself but, in some way she couldn't understand, a little strange. She got out of bed. Miraculously, all her aches and pains had disappeared and she could move freely. Automatically, she went about her usual tasks, cooking and cleaning. In the evening she dozed by the open fire. When night came she went to bed on her old iron bedstead. Days passed but she had no sense of time. Maybe sometimes she wondered why she never got any older or why no one came to see her any more, but it never occurred to her that she was dead.

Through her eyes the house looked as it had done in her day. She saw her own familiar surroundings. From time to time she became aware of the sights and sounds of the living, but these were puzzling sounds and images that didn't belong in her world. She heard unfamiliar voices and saw objects she couldn't understand. What was that box with the moving pictures? What was that machine, so unlike her washing tub, that spun the clothes round and round?

Years came and went. The house changed hands several times. Some of the occupants sensed an uncomfortable presence. Most were oblivious to her. Then Ann and her family moved there. People who are psychic have an energy around them that earthbound spirits sense and it tends to make them more conscious of what is going on. Alice perhaps saw the family and wondered who these intruders were who dared to invade her home. It made her angry. The family, for their part, subconsciously sensed this anger, which is why they were reluctant to go into the room that had been Alice's private territory.

But Alice's lonely ordeal was about to come to an end. When Ann sat in the room that day and meditated she created a mental link between them. Alice began to wake up. This may have made her even more confused. Dimly, she comprehended that something was different, but she couldn't understand what. She still couldn't see anyone from the spirit world.

Then came the day when Ann and I sat together to release her. Our guides gathered around us. Our combined love and compassion penetrated the fog of confusion in which Alice had existed for so long. I imagine that she would have seen a light opening up before her and figures, beings of light, urging her to go towards it. At first she was doubtful, afraid to trust them, but soon they persuaded her. As she moved into the light it was as if a prison door had been flung open. She was swept up on a wave of love and healing and then she was gone, into a world where she would find peace. Ann and I sensed the moment of her departure. And we felt the love fill the room.

The servant and her mistress

There are many spirits like Alice who can be released easily, provided that those on earth treat them with compassion rather than being afraid. Usually they are gone in a minute but, if they are reluctant to leave, it can take longer, and kindness and patience are required. A fascinating account of such a rescue is given by Helen Greaves in her book *The Wheel of Eternity*.

In 1971 Helen moved into a sixteenth-century cottage. She had no idea that it was haunted until one night, when she was reading, she became aware of an old woman sitting in the armchair opposite, staring at her with curiosity and interest. The woman was dressed in a long black dress with a white apron. Helen felt no antagonism from her. She was just a pathetic lost soul.

The woman communicated telepathically that she had been a servant in the large house nearby. She had lived in the cottage alone since her mistress died. It was her own little world – though she accepted Helen without question. In her confused way, she believed that Helen was her lodger, but she accepted her because she was glad of the company.

Over a period of time the woman communicated more of her story. She had hated her mistress, who had been harsh and unfeeling towards her. She had no family of her own. The only person she had loved was the mistress's son, the Boy, as she called him, who had been drowned in the pond. The mistress herself despised this son whom she regarded as an imbecile. The servant was sorry for him and had tried to be a mother to him. Some nights later the Boy himself appeared to Helen, not as a child but as a radiant being of light. He explained to Helen that she herself had been led to the cottage so that she could be an instrument in the rescue of the spirit trapped there.

In her conversations with the old woman Helen tried to discover what was going on in her mind. The woman expressed her pleasure that she no longer had to serve her harsh mistress and could enjoy her cottage in peace.

'It's enough for me. It'll last me out.'

With deliberation I repeated, 'Last you out? What about the end – when you die?'

She was startled. 'Die? That's the end of you, eh?'

'I didn't say so. What about heaven or hell?'

'Don't believe in 'em. Being free and having my own cottage is all the heaven I want.'

So that was it. This was her heaven. No wonder she refuses to become conscious of anything else.

She sat solemnly watching me. 'You're a queer one. Thinking of death and all that.'

'Don't you?'

'No, never. Coffins, and goin' under the ground. Ugh!'

'But we all have to die sometime.'

She was getting annoyed. 'You do keep on so about dying.'

'Do you believe that some part of you lives on?'

'There you go again,' with exasperation. 'No, I don't.'

'But suppose you do live on after death,' I persisted.

Her little face closed up. 'I'll wait till it comes to it to find out.'

Trying to make my thought casual I sent out, 'Perhaps you won't have to wait long.'

She stared at me and I could feel anger rising in her. 'Well, that's a fine thing! Not long, eh? You'll be telling me that I *am* dead next.'

'Are you?'

'No I ain't. If I were would I be sitting 'ere talking to you?'

The old woman concluded that her 'tenant' must be odd to harbour such thoughts and asked Helen if she would like her to call a doctor. Helen seized upon this as a way of making the woman aware of her condition and asked her to do so. But the woman became confused.

'Where ... where will I get one?'

'You don't know a doctor round here?'

'I ain't seen one for years. I don't see folk much these days.' She hesitated, as if caught into some dim remembrance of other times.

'You don't really see anybody, do you?' I probed.

She seemed to stand up with a jerky movement and drew herself to her full five feet of height. 'Why should I? I've got all I want.'

Helen asked her again to call a doctor. She could see that the difficulty of this was worrying the woman. For the first time, she was beginning to sense that something was wrong. Puzzled, she disappeared and came back a few days later. She admitted that she hadn't been able to find a doctor. She couldn't even find the village. She was confused and frightened. Her illusory world was beginning to crumble but still she couldn't accept the truth.

'You're not trying to tell me I'm dead, are you? Dead? I'm alive! I'm talking to you, ain't I? 'Ow could I be dead? It's you.' She seemed to tremble, so that her image in my mind quivered, and became indistinct. 'I remember now. You kept talking about death before.' Now terror enveloped her; she appeared to my inner sight to fade away into a mist. 'That's it! *You're dead!* You must be a ghost!'

The Boy came to Helen many times. Because the servant had been kind to him when he was alive he wanted to help her, but he also wanted to help the mistress, his mother. He explained what had happened to both of them after their deaths. The mistress was not haunting the earth plane; however, because of her cruel treatment of him and her cold, unfeeling nature she had been unable to progress. The servant had been so attached to her little cottage, which had been all she ever desired for herself, that she was unable to leave.

One night both spirits were brought to Helen together. In her inner vision, she saw that the mistress did not at first recognise the boy she had despised as the brilliant being now before her. She accepted his forgiveness and that of the servant she had treated so harshly and, reconciled, they went into the light together.

Why spirits become earthbound

It is interesting to speculate as to why a few spirits become earthbound while the vast majority do not. Simply put, death is a shift in consciousness from the earthly to the spiritual dimension. In the normal way, as soon as a person leaves the physical body they make this shift, easily and automatically. They see loved ones coming to meet them and, though they may be amazed to find themselves still alive, they adjust quickly and enter the world that is waiting for them.

Spirits who become earthbound do not make this shift. Their consciousness remains firmly anchored to the physical dimension. Therefore, the spirit world is invisible to them just as it is to us, and those in the spirit world who are trying to reach them cannot make contact. Obviously, they cannot re-enter the physical world – but they cannot enter the spirit world either, so they are trapped in limbo between the two.

In some instances it is very hard to understand the reason for a spirit's earthbound condition – just as, in this life, it is hard to understand why one person may lead a charmed existence while another suffers endless misfortunes for which, apparently, they are not to blame. No doubt the root cause lies deep in the inner self of the spirit concerned and is between them and God. What we can say with some certainty, however, is that becoming earthbound is not a punishment for misdeeds done on earth. It has more to do with spiritual ignorance than with morality.

A person who had knowledge of life after death is most unlikely to become earthbound. They die in the expectation of finding themselves in another world so it comes as no surprise to them. Likewise, spiritually minded individuals rarely have any difficulty in adjusting to the transition. Even if the manner of their death is traumatic, their minds are already attuned to the spiritual dimension and they immediately feel at home there. By 'spiritually minded', I mean those who cultivate qualities of love and compassion for others, kindness and generosity, not necessarily those who are religious in any conventional sense. These people might choose to spend time after their passing staying close to surviving relatives in order to give them support and comfort, but they are remaining close because they want to, not because they cannot move on.

However, a person who was completely materialistic in their outlook, with no thought of anything in life beyond money and possessions, might become earthbound because they were so attached to these things that they could not tear themselves away. Like Alice, they might create for themselves a dream world in which they thought they were continuing their earthly lives.

If, at some point, they realised that they were dead, the spiritual dimension would still hold no attraction for them. They would prefer to remain close to the things they valued, though frustrated that they couldn't enjoy them any more and perhaps resenting those to whom their possessions had passed. A miser, for instance, might resent the person who had inherited his money and hover around him, angry yet powerless to do anything about it.

Searching for loved ones

Some spirits become stuck because they are searching for loved ones who have died. These loved ones may in fact be present but, because of the earthbound spirit's state of consciousness, it cannot see them. An example of this, given in *True Hauntings* by the American parapsychologist Hazel Denning, shows how tedious such an existence can be.

Raymond, an employee in a radio studio in San Bernadino, California, often heard loud sounds when he was working in the studio at night. He was reluctant to speak of this to his colleagues for fear of ridicule, but one day, in the presence of the entire office staff, a cassette floated up from a shelf and landed gently on the floor. Raymond sought help from Hazel Denning, who visited the premises accompanied by a medium named Gertrude Hall. The medium established contact with a spirit called Harvey, who was amazed that at last someone could see him. He communicated telepathically that the building had once been a duplex (apartment) where he had lived. He was still there waiting there for his son, who had been reported missing during the war but whom he was convinced would one day return.

When Harvey was asked why he moved tapes around and frightened people he replied, 'Do you realise how boring it is just sitting around here all the time waiting for my son?'

To pass the time, he had experimented to see what he could do to get the attention of the people in the studio, and he was amused to watch their reactions. The medium explained to him that he didn't have to stay in the studio and that if he would open his mind to the spiritual dimension, he might find his son there. Harvey was sceptical. Since he believed that the physical world was the only reality, he could not countenance his own death. However, he was persuaded to go. When they checked with Raymond a week later, he reported that the studio was back to normal.

Fixed beliefs and habits

Beliefs instilled by organised religion can become so deeply embedded in the consciousness that they remain after death. Such spirits may easily become confused if they find that the world they have entered is not what they were taught to expect. A Christian who was certain that he was going to heaven would perhaps be puzzled and disappointed at seeing no angels with harps. Someone who was convinced that he would sleep in the tomb until the Day of Judgement might enter a self-induced slumber from which it would be hard for the rescuers to awaken him.

Fear can also be an important factor. Some spirits are afraid to leave the place where they used to live and to move forward because they think they are going to be punished or sent to hell. In fact, there is no such fate awaiting them, but their ingrained belief and sense of guilt keeps them imprisoned.

There are accounts of spirits who remain earthbound for hundreds of years because they died without receiving absolution from a priest or were buried in unconsecrated ground. These things are not important from the point of view of the spirit world but the spirit is still held in the mindset of its earthly life. If the spirit believes that it needs the blessing of the church, then indeed it cannot be at peace without that blessing. In order to release such spirits, the rescuers bring to them a spirit who was a priest on earth because the earthbound spirit recognises the authority represented by such a figure.

Then we have spirits like Alice and the servant in Helen Greaves's home. A great many earthbound spirits are of this type. Their minds are so set in the dull routine of their everyday lives that they continue, by force of habit, to live in the same way as before. This is all they know, and just as in life they never raised their thoughts to anything beyond, so after death they never expand their horizons.

'Bad' spirits

The most troublesome of earthbound spirits are those like the man in the students' flat. They are trapped because of their ignorance and they don't want to learn or progress – they prefer to hang around the earth because that is where they are most comfortable. Like that particular spirit, most of them are not as bad as they first seem and are really just lost souls desperately in need of a little love and attention. But, as I will now go on to describe, they sometimes have an amazing amount of power and can cause havoc for the poor victims whose houses they inhabit.

5

Troublesome Tenants

A troublesome spirit is like a child in a tantrum, stomping around and making a nuisance so that someone will take notice of them. Usually, it works. Such spirits can make the lives of the people living in the house a misery, not only by physical manifestations but by intruding into their minds and causing them to act in ways that are out of character.

In the last chapter I wrote about the old lady in Ann's house – Alice, as I called her – who was dealt with successfully. Some time later, Ann approached me again. Her family now had another spirit, one who was far less friendly. All Ann's sons were aware of this character. Philip, who was very sensitive, complained of the 'old man' in his bedroom who disturbed him. One of her other boys had opened the loft hatch in order to go into the roof space and had felt something 'whoosh' past him, breathing heavily in his ear. He was so shocked that he fell off the ladder!

I called on Ann a few days later, and she told me what had been happening. 'Since we freed the old woman, the house has been clear. But just lately we've all felt that there was a man here creating a tense atmosphere. I tried sending out light to him but he didn't go away. Philip was getting really frightened.'

Ann realised that the spirit was affecting them all. The children usually got on well. Occasionally they squabbled, as all children do, but recently their squabbling had taken on a vicious nature which was quite unlike any of them. The spirit seemed to have latched on to Philip most of all. Though usually quiet and peaceful, he had got into trouble at school for hitting another child, something he had never done before. Another, highly sceptical member of the family was also affected. Like many people, he enjoyed a glass of wine with a meal occasionally but never drank to excess. Yet since the spirit had been in the house he had been drinking far more than usual and couldn't understand why.

When I made contact with the spirit I found that, unlike Alice, the old man was quite well aware of what he was doing. I asked the guides where he had come from. They told me that he had no connection with the house. He had arrived with a visitor who had been drinking in a pub.

The spirit was not easy to shift. Because he was bitter and angry, he was aggravating the small disagreements that arose between the children, which was why they were behaving so badly. He had been an alcoholic, and this influence was causing Ann's relative to drink. Ann and I tried persuasion but the spirit refused to budge. Eventually the guides took a hand. They do, on occasions, evict troublesome spirits to prevent them from harming the living. They are quite firm about this. It is what I call, metaphorically speaking, taking them by the scruff of the neck! When this was done, needless to say, everything in the family returned to normal.

The lady in brown

Psychical researchers love having a ghost to investigate and will often travel long distances to look into what they think is a promising case, but sometimes they fail to recognise psychic phenomena occurring under their very noses. The distinguished researcher and writer Montague Keen, known to his friends as Monty, died in 2004. He had spent a lifetime studying parapsychology and was respected throughout the world for his knowledge. However, when his wife Veronica told him that they had a haunting in their north London home he refused to believe it. Veronica told me the story.

'We knew as soon as we saw the house that this was the one. When we first looked at it, it was a building site! We had to do a lot of work to get it the way we wanted it. When we moved in, I was conscious that I was not alone. I saw a lady three or four times. She was always dressed in brown. She wasn't solid. We were always having problems with the electricity and water. We called in electricians and plumbers so many times but as soon as they had put the fault right it would go wrong again. But Monty wouldn't believe it was a haunting.

'Monty had fixed a steel wine rack to the wall in the garage. One day he went into the garage and found that it had been ripped off the wall. The bottles were all over the floor. Some of them were broken. That convinced him! We called in our friends Michael and Jenny Ayres, who are mediums.

'On the day they were due to come, I was behaving in a strange way, being really nasty to Monty. I loved Monty so much and I would never have spoken to him like that. I could hear myself saying these things but it didn't seem to be me speaking. I was shouting at him, "I'm trapped in this bloody house. I can't get out!" It was an awful feeling. Monty thought I had gone off my head. He was really worried about me. It took a while for him to accept that it wasn't me.

'Then Michael and Jenny arrived. Jenny contacted the spirit and told us that her name was Winifred Joyce and that she had lived in the house. In her confused state of mind she thought she was still living there and that Monty and I were tenants. She had hated alcohol. She said, through Jenny, "I will not have drink in this house!" That was why she had torn the rack off the wall.

'Winifred was angry because we were altering her home. She said, "They've destroyed my nook!" I didn't understand what she meant at the time.

'Jenny talked to her, telling her to go towards the light. I reacted because I could feel what the spirit was feeling, and she didn't want to go. Jenny said, "You'll see your family." Then a change came over the woman. She said, "There's Tom!" And I felt her going away.

'Later, I spoke to the neighbours. They told me that the house had been occupied by a woman who had always worn brown. There was a corner of the room where she used to sit which she had called her "nook".'

Monty and Veronica thought that their house was free of spirits but Veronica had an unpleasant surprise in store. Three weeks later, she again detected a presence.

'I said to Monty, "We've got another one!" This time I felt that it was a man. There was trouble with the plumbing again. The tiles in the bathroom were cut as if with a powerful tool. I told Monty, "We've got to get Jenny and Michael back."'

Once again, Veronica found herself behaving strangely, as if the spirit was taking her over. 'Monty wanted to go out into the garden. I was crying, clinging to him. "Please don't leave me!" He said, "I'm only just outside. You can see me from the window." He told me to lie down but I said, "I mustn't close my eyes." I was terrified! My legs were freezing cold up to my waist.

'When Jenny came, she picked up that the man was called Alf. He had been in water up to his waist, desperately trying to hold on. Eventually he couldn't hold on any longer and he drowned. Apparently, he had lived and died somewhere nearby. He was walking past our house when he saw a light and knew that there were people there who could help him.

'Jenny was able to release him. Some time later, he came back through another medium to thank me and to say how happy he was.'

Poltergeists

Destructive spirits who throw things around are called poltergeists. The word is German and means 'noisy spirit'. Poltergeists have probably been studied more extensively than any other type of psychic phenomenon but there is still much we don't understand about them. Some researchers claim that they are a different species from 'ordinary' ghosts but I have not found this to be the case. Whenever it has been possible to contact them they have proved to be essentially like any other earthbound spirit. It is just that they are making their presence known in a very obvious way.

Poltergeist activity can vary in strength, from mild cases where footsteps and other noises are heard and small objects are moved to violent examples which are terrifyingly malevolent. Fortunately, these are extremely rare and I personally have never encountered anything really scary. I suppose, however, it depends upon how easily frightened you are. I have known people who were thrilled to have a ghost able to produce footsteps and open and close doors, but anyone might be nervous if their furniture took to moving around of its own accord, as happened to one of my clients.

The farm labourer

Pam was thrilled with her house when she first moved into it. Though conveniently near the town, it was one of a small cluster of cottages in an open area of what had once been farmland. She was not deterred by the fact that it needed renovation and decided to save money by doing as much of the work as she could herself, only calling in builders for the jobs she couldn't manage.

However, after a few days she became aware of a presence. The dogs detected it too, becoming restless and uneasy. Pam found the bedroom where she slept cold and depressing. She heard noises in there at night and the coat hangers in the wardrobe would rattle. One day when she had been out, she returned to find that her heavy chest of drawers had been dragged across the floor.

But if this wasn't bad enough, her problems really started

when she began to convert the small lobby downstairs into a shower room. Faults developed with the plumbing that the builder couldn't account for. Every time he put something right, it would go wrong again soon afterwards. This caused considerable delay, but at last the job was nearing completion and the plumber put up the tiles. But no sooner had he left the room than there was a resounding crash. Pam rushed downstairs to see what had happened, to find that the tiles had been ripped from the wall.

The plumber hurried away, never to be seen again. But Pam was made of sterner stuff. A strong-minded woman, she had considerable psychic ability and she wasn't going to let a spirit drive her out of her house, so she called me. I sat in the bedroom, tuning in. The spirit whose presence I sensed was a middle-aged man, scruffily dressed, his trousers tied round the waist with a piece of string. He had been a labourer on the farm that had been there in his day. This had been his cottage. He didn't like this woman who had taken it over, and he wanted her out.

It is important for me, as it is for any medium who does rescue work, to have complete trust and confidence in my guides to protect me. A spirit who can strip tiles off a wall is not to be taken lightly. But the guides told me that neither Pam nor I was in any danger. In very human terms, they helped me to understand what was going on. The man had been very lonely at the end of his life. His family had either died before him or left him and he had no friends. Perhaps because of his vicious temper – which he was still exhibiting – no one wanted to know him. He had deteriorated into a state of depression and his only comfort had been in drink. All his thoughts had been centred upon the dull routine of his life. He had no concept of any existence beyond death. He had died with a mind full of anger and bitterness towards everyone around him, and after death he had remained fixed in that mental state.

I asked the guides whether he realised that he was dead. I was told that in some dim way he did understand, but he was confused. Part of his mind was in the present day, objecting to the changes Pam was making to 'his' house – but part of him was still stuck in his own times. I had a mental impression of him standing by the window, looking out over what, when he was alive, must have been cultivated fields, and I felt sorry for him.

Speaking to him in my mind, I told him that he didn't have to stay in the house, that there was somewhere better for him to go. He seemed touched by this kindness and concern. I don't suppose anyone had been kind to him when he was alive. I said that the guides had come to help him and that he should go into the light. As I did so, I sensed that he saw a light opening up before him and a woman – perhaps a wife or daughter – coming across the fields to meet him.

All his anger disappeared. 'Well, I never!' I heard him say in my mind, as though he could scarcely believe what he was seeing. Then he went – but just before leaving he added, 'Tell the lady I'm sorry I frightened her.'

Psychic energy

In this instance, like many others, the spirit was not malicious. He was simply frustrated and calling for help in the only way he knew. It was fortunate that Pam was understanding and, once she was made aware of his plight, wanted to help him. But she was amazed at the amount of energy he was able to summon up and she wanted to know where he got this energy from.

This is one of the mysteries of poltergeist cases. I put the question to the writer Guy Lyon Playfair, a leading expert on poltergeists, who frankly admitted that no one knows the answer. He told me, 'What we do know is that poltergeists do things we can't do, such as levitate human beings, make solid objects go through doors and walls (or appear to), throw things in straight trajectories and move objects that are too heavy or large for a single person to move. They do things that are absolutely impossible in terms of physics and biology as we know them – and they can keep it up for hours.'

It seems clear that one of the main sources of energy for poltergeists is that which they draw from the people living in the house. Anyone who is psychic, even if they don't recognise that they have psychic ability, emanates the sort of power spirits can use. People like this find that psychic or poltergeist activity breaks out wherever they go. Children, who are often naturally psychic, are another power source. The house itself may hold residual energy from past people and events.

Negative ley lines, water and underground springs have been suggested as possible sources of energy. Overhead power cables may be another factor. Guy is of the opinion that although water or power lines may make a poltergeist more energetic, they are not enough in themselves to provide the fuel for the manifestations. He points out that nearly every house has power cables or underground water nearby, but we don't find poltergeists all over the place!

He does, however, feel – and I completely agree on this

point – that whenever there is poltergeist activity in a house, there is tension within the family. The troublesome spirits somehow draw upon this tension. They may play upon the emotions of the people in the house, thus making the tension worse and giving themselves greater power.

Poltergeists and children

I mentioned that children are an energy source, and it has been observed that poltergeist activity tends to centre upon children who are at the age of puberty. A favourite theory of parapsychologists is that children of this age generate a lot of unconscious kinetic energy. This is particularly true if the child is harbouring suppressed anger or resentment. The phenomena are thought to be a manifestation of their suppressed emotions.

It is true that, in some cases, once the child concerned has been given counselling or been treated by a psychiatrist who has succeeded in resolving their hidden conflicts, the manifestations have stopped. This is seen by parapsychologists as proving that the phenomena were produced by the child. As I believe, however, it merely indicates that once the child's inner turmoil was settled, he or she no longer gave off such disruptive energy – and therefore there was no power for the spirit to use.

Guy's comment on the kinetic energy theory is that it is just not sufficient to account for the feats of which a poltergeist is capable. He believes – and mediums would agree with him – that children do indeed emit energy, but that poltergeist activity occurs only because there is an entity around who uses and manipulates that energy.

He prefers to refer to poltergeists as 'entities' rather than spirits, as the word 'entity' does not necessarily imply a surviving individual. But he acknowledges that they do seem to have some sort of intelligence. He states: 'Poltergeists act as if they were independent entities, so they probably are.' He cites the well-known case of the Enfield poltergeist which he investigated in 1977. This involved a family living in north London who were plagued with vicious and terrifying manifestations that continued for many months. Janet, the child who appeared to be the epicentre of the activity, repeatedly described being picked up by 'cold hands' and thrown or pulled out of bed. She regularly spoke at great length in the voice of an adult man, sometimes making claims that later turned out to be true, such as that he had gone blind and died in his armchair. This was exactly what had happened to the previous owner of the house – but it was completely unknown to Janet.

Plumbing and electricity

A feature both of Pam's case and that of the spirit in Monty and Veronica's home was the trouble that occurred with the plumbing. This is very common. There is some connection between psychic energy and water – and that is another mystery. Puddles of water sometimes occur where poltergeists are evident, and the curious nature of these puddles is that they have sharp outlines rather than spreading out over the floor as water normally would. Guy Lyon Playfair explains this by saying that the power used by the spirit is concentrated in small areas, like 'footballs' of energy. When these burst, the energy condenses – hence the puddle.

Electrical energy is also somehow connected with psychic manifestations. A very common feature of haunted houses is interference with electrical equipment, such as lights that flicker and televisions that change channels or switch themselves on or off. Investigators at the scene of a haunting frequently complain that their equipment malfunctions or refuses to work at all.

Guy comments, 'Poltergeists have a fairly limited repertoire and I assume they do what they find easiest. You don't have to do much to put an electrical device out of action. Also, there is a lot of electricity around so any new source of energy is bound to interfere with it.'

Poltergeists in the bedroom

Poltergeists seem to have a fascination with bedrooms and bedroom furniture. In one of the most frequent manifestations, the bed is shaken or people have the bedclothes pulled off them – or are even thrown out of bed on to the floor! This may be because as we fall asleep and the spirit body temporarily leaves the physical, we give off energy. Many psychic experiences take place in that halfway stage between sleeping and waking.

I have only once had an encounter of this kind. I was staying with a friend who was renting a remote cottage in the country. She had made up a bed for me in a downstairs room. Just as I was falling asleep, I felt the bedclothes being tugged by an invisible hand. I sat up and put the light on. I couldn't see anything, but the room was icy cold. This was before I knew anything about earthbound spirits, so I said a prayer and tried to go back to sleep. But the same thing happened again. It was a very uncomfortable night. In the morning, my friend casually remarked that she had known the cottage was haunted but hadn't thought to mention it. I don't know who the ghost was – but I didn't wait to find out!

John and Sharon, relatives of one of my clients, live in Staffordshire, and they purchased a house which had previously belonged to an elderly couple. The wife had died in the house, and the husband had moved to a nursing home where he too died not long afterwards. For a year after they moved in John and Sharon experienced nothing untoward but when they began making alterations to the house, Sharon started feeling extremely nervous and uncomfortable and didn't like being there alone. The dogs, too, were behaving strangely and seemed uneasy but, for protection, Sharon had them sleeping in the bedroom with her.

One night she and John woke up to find that all the drawers in a chest of drawers had been opened. A few days later, they returned home after visiting friends to see that the chest – which was a heavy piece of furniture – had been turned round so that it was facing the wall. It was in a confined space, and there was no way that it could have been moved like this without lifting it up clear of the bed.

Sharon was nervous about calling in a medium. But John felt intuitively that the old man who had lived there was responsible. He consulted his sister, who had some experience of psychic matters, and her advice was simple: 'Tell him to go away!' This John did, and they had no further trouble. The spirit perhaps decided that he wasn't welcome and left. But I wished that I, or a local medium, had been given the opportunity to release him.

Grave's End

Having one earthbound spirit in your house is bad enough, but if you have a whole host of them they can drive you to a nervous breakdown. Elaine Mercado, in her book *Grave's End*, recounts her extraordinary experiences of living in a haunted house in the appropriately named Grave's End district of Brooklyn.

The old and unkempt house was owned by a middle-aged couple. It came with a pair of sitting tenants, the husband's parents, who lived in a flat in the basement. Desperate to find somewhere to live after months of house hunting and relieved to find somewhere they could afford, Elaine, her husband, and daughters Karin and Christine ignored the house's spooky atmosphere and moved in.

The elderly couple, however, refused for a long time to move out or to let Elaine explore their living quarters. It wasn't until they finally left that she was able to have a look at the basement. To her surprise, she found that it took up less than a third of the length of the house. She was informed by neighbours that the house had been moved in its entirety from a site round the corner. The other two-thirds of the basement had never been dug out but had been left as what the family called a 'dirt room', an empty cavity hardly big enough to stand up in, sealed off by a couple of doors.

Elaine used the basement as a laundry room, but whenever she was there she had the uncomfortable sensation of being watched. She was afraid to be alone there, and began hearing strange noises in various parts of the house. But, not being a believer in the supernatural, she put these things to the back of her mind. Then she began to have suffocating dreams. She knew they were something different from the well-known phenomenon of sleep paralysis – she would be fully conscious, but frightened beyond reason, and unable to move because of a pressure on her chest. The pressure would spread until it covered her whole body. At the same time she had a sensation that someone was in the room with her. When she checked with her daughters she found that they had experienced the same dreams.

As time went on, the phenomena in the house mounted, while there was a growing sense of tension. There were footsteps, foul smells, balls of light and a mist that came and went. Elaine had to acknowledge that something was very wrong with the house, but she didn't know where to turn for help. The situation continued for ten years, a period during which, moreover, she was going through a divorce from her husband. Sometimes there would be quiet periods in the house when nothing happened, then it would all start up again. The nightmares became steadily worse. She was exhausted by sleeplessness and fear. Her daughters were affected too and often they all slept, fully dressed, with the lights on. Still she told no one outside the family about what was going on.

Eventually, she found a new partner who listened, incredulously but with sympathy, as she confided in him about the haunting. He contacted the parapsychologist Hans Holzer, who had investigated many poltergeist cases. Holzer visited the house with a medium, Marisa Anderson, who finally solved the mystery. Sensing immediately that the focus of the disturbance was in the basement, she opened the doors to the dirt room and sat inside. She told the family that she was sensing five people who had been buried alive there in the mid-1800s. They had been building something like a mine that ran through the neighbourhood under the basements of the houses. A collapse had occurred, either deliberately or through someone's neglect, and they were slowly suffocated to death. Some of them had taken five days to die – yet they refused to believe that their lives had ended. They were confused, lost and angry, and were pleading for help.

The medium explained that they had been trying to communicate their feelings as best they could. The sensations of pressure and suffocation that Elaine and her daughters had experienced had been what the spirits suffered as they died. This, at last, was the explanation for the nightmares.

The medium told the spirits to go to the light, repeating the phrase over and over until they understood and began to respond. For three hours, she talked to them until the last had left, then she cleansed the whole house. For Elaine and her daughters, their troubles were finally at an end.

The family in this case suffered for so long not only because of the severity of the haunting but because they didn't realise that they could call upon the services of a medium to deal with it. Unless you are extremely unlucky, you will never experience anything of such a terrifying nature in your home. However, if anything inexplicable is happening where you live, you may by now be wondering, 'Is my house haunted?' I am now going to tell you how to decide if it is and, if so, what to do about it.

6

Is Your House Haunted?

Is your house haunted? If you have a poltergeist you will be in no doubt of the fact. Even the most hardened sceptic would find it hard to explain away a chest of drawers that moves by itself or a wine rack that is ripped from a wall. Perhaps you have felt a presence, heard strange noises or seen something disturbing. In that case, you may well have a resident spirit. But what if there is nothing specific you can pin down, just a vague sense that the house doesn't 'feel right'? Then there may be some other reason.

I mentioned in Chapter 3 a number of factors that should be considered. Let me remind you of these.

Natural causes

Each house, especially an old one, has its characteristic noises, caused by the woodwork, by pipes expanding and contracting and the like. Areas of cold may be due to an ill-fitting window. If there is a nasty smell, inspect the drains! This may sound obvious, but it is surprising how many people don't think to check these things out first. Nevertheless, you need to trust your intuition. If you have done all this but your inner sense tells you that there is something wrong with your house – then there probably is.

Negative energy

As I have explained, this can emanate from a number of possible sources. It may be worth making enquiries with neighbours about the previous occupants of the property. (This will probably need to be done discreetly. The suggestion that your house may be haunted is not something you can drop casually into the conversation!) Moreover, be honest enough to acknowledge and tackle any disharmony, tensions or emotional difficulties that may exist in your family.

If you have eliminated these possibilities, consider whether the problem may go back further in time. It is worth doing some detective work to explore the history of the house and the site. Look in your local library for reference books giving information about anything that may have happened on that spot in the past, and which could have left an energy trace behind.

Negative earth energy

What about negative earth energy? Unless you have some expertise, this is hard to detect. Earth energies can be both positive and negative. Places of positive energy have a good feel about them. They are invigorating and conducive to spiritual activities such as healing and meditation. The veil between the worlds is thinner in such places, so they facilitate spirit communication. Should your house be in such an area, then you are fortunate, as it will probably feel happy and harmonious. Any psychic activity that might occur will be of a pleasant nature; for example, it may be possible to sense the presence of loving friends and relatives from the spirit world.

However, a house located on a negative energy site never feels comfortable. It always seems dark and gloomy, no matter how bright the décor or how much sunlight comes in. The people living there often feel tired and drained and may be prone to minor illnesses and infections, or more serious health problems. They may experience bad luck and complain that nothing in their lives ever seems to go right. If this sounds like a description of your house, negative energy may be the reason.

Space clearing

Whatever the cause of the problem, it is a good idea to start by space clearing – in other words, cleansing and purifying the energy of the house in order to dispel negativity. This always gives a house a brighter, fresher feeling. You may find that it solves the problem completely, in which case there is nothing further you need to do. If not, space clearing is a good preliminary to any further work that may have to be carried out.

First, on a practical level, give the house a thorough spring clean. If necessary, redecorate. Get rid of any clutter you are hoarding. For further suggestions and techniques you might like to consult some of the excellent books on space clearing that are now available. I have included a couple of titles in the list of recommended reading at the end of this book.

For further help, you should consider calling in a feng shui practitioner (see Resources at the end of the book). Feng shui works with the subtle energy fields of the house and the site. A good feng shui practitioner will be able to determine the cause of the negativity and will rebalance the energy. He or she will also be able to locate negative earth energy lines that are having an adverse effect on the property. These can sometimes be reversed. In addition, you will be given advice as to the positioning of furniture, the use of specific colours in decorations and other ways in which you can improve the harmony of your home.

Clearing the energy yourself

You can clear the energy of the house still further by using the simple technique I am going to describe. I have taught this to many people and it is very effective in bringing about a subtle but noticeable change. All it requires is that you use your intuition and focus the power of your mind, and that you call upon the forces of light to assist you.

There are various tools you may find helpful to assist in your task, although they are not essential. These are:

✦ Candles (and matches, of course!). Candles are an age-old symbol of light and purity.

✦ Incense or aromatherapy oil. Again, these are good for

clearing and purifying. Sandalwood is particularly suitable.

✦ Smudge sticks. These are an ancient device used by Native American Indians. A smudge stick is a bundle of sage twigs which, when lighted, give off a sweet-smelling smoke.

✦ Room sprays. Many New Age shops sell a variety of room sprays. Choose one which is specifically designed for cleansing.

✦ Bells. You can use a hand bell or a Tibetan singing bowl. Bowls are played by rubbing a small stick or wand around the outside of the rim. They create a very beautiful and penetrating sound.

Decide which of these tools, if any, you are going to use. Select those which most appeal to you – you don't need to use them all. When you have got everything together you are ready to start.

Exercise: To clear the energy of your house

✦ Choose a time when you can be sure of not being disturbed. Allow an hour or two. If other members of your family are sympathetic you can invite them to take part with you. If not, do it when they are out!

✦ Start with a prayer. Whether you pray to God, to Jesus or another spiritual master is entirely a matter of your personal belief. You may prefer simply to focus on the light or to call upon the angels. What is essential is that you send out your thoughts to whatever source of goodness, wisdom and power feels right to you. If you are aware of spirit guides or guardians, call upon them also.

✦ Begin with the room which you sense is most in need of clearing. If you are not sure about this, choose the room you and your family use most. Light your candle if you are using one, or burn your oil, incense or smudge stick.

✦ Stand in the middle of the room. Take a few deep breaths to relax yourself. Try to sense the energy of the room. In what way does it seem disturbed? For instance, does it feel heavy or disharmonious? Does it make you feel restless or uneasy? You are now going to change that energy, using the power of your thoughts and the light which you have invoked by your prayers.

✦ Visualise a golden light that comes down from above your head. Imagine that you are breathing in this light. Hold it within yourself and feel it filling your entire being with joy and strength.

✦ Now breathe out and, as you do so, imagine that you are radiating this golden light all around you. It spreads out to fill the whole of the room from floor to ceiling, going into all the corners. Go around the room with your bell or singing bowl, sounding it first in the centre of the room and then going into every corner.

✦ When you are satisfied you have done all that is necessary (and you will have to use your intuition in this), go round the whole house carrying out the same procedure in each room. Finish by visualising a golden light above the whole house and see it coming down like a powerful ray.

This ray surrounds the outside of the house, sealing it and keeping it safe and protected.

✦ Having finished your ritual, walk round the house again. Stand still in each room in turn and sense how the energy has changed.

You may need to repeat this ritual two or three times to make sure that it has worked. In many cases it is all that is needed to transform a depressing, uncomfortable house into a happy, harmonious one. However, it is important to bear in mind that the incense, bells or any other aids you use are no more than tools or symbols. They have no power in themselves. What brings about the clearing is the power of your mind, the purity of your intention and the strength of your prayers.

Is there an earthbound spirit present?

Cleansing a house will usually dispel any ghosts, since these are in reality only a form of residual energy. It will not harm any earthbound spirits who may be there. It fact, it will help because it brings light into the house, which may be enough to release them.

But perhaps you have tried all the above measures and you still feel that the house is not clear. Is there an earthbound spirit still present who needs a little more help? This is possible. The signs can be subtle. I have already spoken about some of these. But, to refresh your memory, here is a list of things to look out for.

Physical indications

Noises

Noises in haunted houses are extremely varied and can range from little bangs and clicks to quite loud thumps, though I have never heard rattling chains! The sound of breaking glass that was heard in my parents' house is a typical example. I remember on one occasion returning home from a shopping trip with my mother and hearing such loud footsteps from the bedroom that I rushed upstairs, fearing that we had burglars. Of course, there was no one there. I was considerably shaken, but my mother was so used to this happening that she calmly shrugged her shoulders and went to put the kettle on.

Feelings of cold

Haunted houses have a particular kind of coldness about them. It produces a shivery feeling, different from ordinary cold and instantly recognisable to anyone who deals with ghosts. It may be localised in one room or one part of the house, and this area is the focal point of the activity. This coldness cannot be traced to draughts from doors or windows, and no amount of heating will ever make the room warm or cosy.

Smells

Smells can be pleasant or unpleasant, and relate to something with which the spirit would have been familiar in life. Common odours are cigarettes or tobacco, flowers or perfume. Strangely, these smells often manifest suddenly and disappear again just as quickly, rather than fading gradually as a normal smell would do.

Nasty smells can be hard to get rid of. I was once called to a large Victorian house that had been converted into flats. The young woman who lived on the ground floor was constantly plagued by the sort of smell associated with an old person who is incontinent. No matter how much she cleaned and disinfected, the smell remained. I traced the cause to a former servant in the house, and once he was released, the smell went with him.

Movement of objects

We all put things down from time to time and forget where we have put them. This is easily explained by forgetfulness or old age. But if things frequently go missing or disappear altogether and you are sure no one in the house is responsible, it may be a ghost playing tricks. The simplest remedy is to order them, aloud if you wish, to bring the objects back. It is surprising how often a firm command works!

Objects are hardly ever seen in the process of moving. Spirits behave rather like naughty children who stop what they are doing as soon as they know they are being observed. It takes a lot of power to shift heavy objects such as pieces of furniture. Fortunately, not many spirits can manage this!

Interference with electrical equipment

I have mentioned the connection between psychic energy and electricity. It is very common for lights to flicker or to be turned on or off. There may also be interference with computers or televisions. This may, for the spirit, be one of the easiest ways in which it can let people know it is there.

I have never noticed flickering lights in my home or had any inexplicable problems with the computer. However, I have noticed something interesting in the room where I give sittings. On many occasions, sitters who come to see me armed with tape recorders to record the session find that the machine won't work. I have lost count of the times I have heard people say, 'That's funny – it was working perfectly before I left home!'

Intangible indications

Feeling a presence

Spirits are far more likely to be sensed than seen and feeling a presence is, in my experience, the most common indication of a haunting. Often, people say 'I never see anything but I just know there's someone there.' They may try to convince themselves that they're imagining it but deep down they know they're not. It reminds me of a poem I used to recite as a child:

> As I was going up the stair
> I met a man who wasn't there.
> He wasn't there again today,
> Oh, how I wish he'd go away!

The presence may be a quiet one in the background or there may be a more intrusive sense of being watched – embarrassing if your spirit has taken up residence in the bathroom! The sensation may be tactile. Though I have never heard anyone say they were grabbed by an icy hand, I have heard many people complain that they felt a touch on the arm, sometimes quite definite, sometimes so light it was like a breeze or a draught. Occasionally voices may be heard, but these are generally so indistinct that it is impossible to make out the words.

Sightings

If you see a spirit, it is usually as a shadow. Or you may catch sight of something out of the corner of your eye, but when you turn to look, it has vanished. There is a very good reason for this. The retina contains two types of cells, rods and cones. The cones see in colour; the rods give us peripheral vision, mainly in black and white. Our peripheral vision is more sensitive and operates as the light fades – therefore ghosts are seen out of the corner of the eye, often at dusk, and appear to be colourless.

Some sightings do, however, take place in full colour and in broad daylight. The spirit appears absolutely real and solid then, a second later, it has gone. How you see a spirit depends upon how strong your psychic ability is. It is a comforting thought that, even if you do have a clear sighting, it usually happens so quickly that there is no time to be frightened.

Emotional reactions

Earthbound spirits can sap your energy. If your house is haunted you may feel constantly tired and drained. You may pick up other emotions from the spirit such as feelings of depression, fear or anxiety.

The more sensitive you are, the more you are likely to be affected. You can even pick up physical symptoms. One of my clients had a spirit in her house who had been a heavy smoker. She suffered from chest and nasal complaints for which her doctor could find no cause and which were especially troublesome to her, as she was a singer. Once the spirit was released, the symptoms disappeared.

Obviously, any physical or mental symptoms you are experiencing should be checked out by a doctor or alternative health practitioner. But, if there is no obvious reason for them, an earthbound spirit may be at the root of the matter.

You should also watch for any inexplicable changes in behaviour in yourself or other family members. A disruptive spirit can spread disharmony throughout the family, playing on any existing or suppressed anger or resentment and exacerbating disagreements and misunderstandings. Once this process has started to take a hold, it can be hard to approach the problem in a calm, methodical way, since everyone's nerves are on edge.

Children and animals

Every haunting is different. You may have noticed some – probably not all – of the above signs in your house but perhaps you are still a little doubtful. The idea that you have a spirit sharing your living space can be a hard one to take on board. As always, you have to trust your intuition on this. Don't be put off by other household members telling you that you are going off your head!

Listen very carefully to anything young children say, as they are much more sensitive than adults. A child who talks about 'the old man at the top of the stairs' or 'the woman who comes to tuck me in at night' is unlikely to be making it up. Take careful note if your child is having nightmares. Though these may, of course, occur because the child is troubled in some way, it may be that a spirit is disturbing them during their sleep. Also, watch the reactions of animals. It is a well-documented fact – and a feature of countless ghost stories – that a cat or dog will refuse to enter a room that is haunted.

Is it a relative?

Don't forget the possibility that your 'ghost' might be a relative come to visit. Think of deceased family members to whom you were close, perhaps parents or grandparents, and try to sense if it is someone you know. Send out your thoughts to them and ask them, either mentally or aloud, to tell you who they are, and see if you can sense a response. Think too whether anyone among your family and friends has died recently.

If you sense love, peace and happiness emanating from the spirit then they are not earthbound, they are there just because they care about you. They will appreciate it very much if you book a sitting with a medium (they will come with you) in order to give them the opportunity to communicate.

Is it a stranger?

Ask yourself whether your awareness of the spirit began immediately you came to live in the property, or soon afterwards. It may be the spirit of someone who used to live in the house. It could even be someone who was attached to the previous occupants and has been left behind, like the pile of old books in the attic.

Spirits can arrive at any time, brought in by visitors or

family members. Think whether you or anyone living in your house has recently been to a property that may have been haunted. The spirit may have hitched a lift with them then decided to stay with you, finding your house more congenial than its last place of residence. It may have been drifting aimlessly outside and been attracted by your light. It is easy to imagine a homeless person wandering the streets and, finding a house where the lights are on and there is warmth, coming inside and making himself at home.

If you have recently made alterations or carried out renovations to the house, this may have stirred things up. Even those spirits who are in a dreamlike, semi-conscious state can somehow sense that the energy of the house has been disturbed. A spirit like Veronica's brown lady, who is very attached to the house and liked it just the way it was, may object to the changes and leave you in no doubt as to their annoyance.

Should you try to release the spirit yourself?

As you will have realised by now, there are many reasons why a house may have an earthbound spirit in it. Most people are very curious to know who the spirit is, or was. It isn't always possible to discover this but usually it isn't too important to know. All that matters is to release the spirit. You now have to decide whether you are going to attempt the task yourself or whether you need to enlist outside help. Only attempt it yourself under the following conditions:

✦ If you feel sure that the presence is benign
✦ If you have mediumistic ability yourself, or can work with a person who has
✦ If you have no fear of the spirit.

And let me give you a word of warning:

✦ If you feel any element of fear
✦ If you sense any darkness or malice emanating from the spirit
✦ If you are lacking in any psychic awareness

LEAVE WELL ALONE.

Who are you gonna call?

If you decide you need help, please don't think *Ghostbusters*! There is no need to evict the spirit by 'busting' it out of your home. How would you feel if someone attempted to forcibly evict you? Calling in the vicar is probably a waste of time. Should the clergyman be a person with a spiritual understanding rather than someone whose spirituality comes out of a textbook, he may have spiritual guides with him, even if he doesn't know anything about them, and they will be able to do the job. However, most clergymen are of no use at all in these situations. Far better to call in a medium.

The easiest way to find a medium is to enquire at your local Spiritualist church. The address should be listed in the phone book. A number of Spiritualist organisations are listed in the Resources section at the back of this book, and these organisations should be able to put you in touch with a medium in your area. There are also many websites listed under 'Spiritualist churches' or 'mediums'.

Exercise: Releasing an earthbound spirit

If you feel equal to attempting the job yourself, here are some guidelines to follow:

✦ As with the house clearing method described above, find a quiet time and begin with a prayer.

✦ Always ask for protection, just in case (read Chapter 13, Psychic Protection, before you begin).

✦ Speak to the spirit aloud or in your mind. Since spirits can read your thoughts it is unnecessary to speak aloud, but you may find this easier. (There is no need to feel silly talking to apparently empty space – I do it all the time!) Tell the spirit that you are aware of its presence and that you wish to help it.

✦ Keep sending out thoughts of compassion.

✦ Call upon your own guides or loved ones or the rescuers to come to the aid of the spirit. Try to sense the light coming into the room. Keep your kind thoughts centred upon the spirit and tell it to go into the light. Remain alert for any impressions that come into your mind.

✦ After a few minutes you should feel a change in the energy of the room. There will be a lightening of the atmosphere and a sense of relief. When this happens, you will know that the spirit has gone. Say a final prayer and wish it well. Thank the guides who have been working with you.

✦ Do a final visualisation, as in the energy clearing exercise, to clear the room of any residual energy. Using any of the tools I have mentioned will help in this.

✦ Allow a couple of days for the energy to settle down. During this time, try not to think about the spirit. It may still be in the process of adjusting to the change in its conditions and concentrating your thoughts on it may occasionally draw it back.

Can it really be that easy? Yes, it can, and in most cases it is. Even a spirit who may have seemed frightening can be easily released. A client of mine once sought my help because of a strong and seemingly menacing presence in her bedroom. It was a few days before I was able to visit her and, in the meantime, she had moved her bed downstairs and converted the bedroom into a temporary sanctuary where she said prayers and meditated. By the time I arrived, the spirit had gone and the room felt calm and peaceful. I would repeat, however, that if at any time you have any doubt of what to do – whether or not you have been successful – or if you feel frightened or uneasy in any way, don't hesitate to call in a medium.

One last point. You may feel that, if your resident spirit isn't doing any harm, you might as well leave it there. Some people like living in a haunted house and don't want it cleared. Equally, there are spirits who seem quite happy where they are and don't want to go. Generally, however, I would advise that stuck spirits should be encouraged to move on, for their own good. While they are present they can't enter fully into the dimension where they belong or make progress spiritually. It is an act of kindness to set them free.

I have referred many times to spirits going 'into the light'. Where is this light – and what is the world like to which they are taken?

7

Moving Towards the Light

Imagine that you are an earthbound spirit trapped within a house. Everything around you seems dark and gloomy. Like a listless sleepwalker, you wander around from room to room. You know you are alive yet things have changed in a way you don't understand. Your mind is muddled and everything seems confused. There are people in the house who don't belong there – intruders. You try to reach out to them but they don't respond, or perhaps you try to frighten them away.

Then one day, along comes a stranger. This person is different. He can talk to you. He seems to understand. With him you see others, radiant figures. They tell you, 'You don't need to stay here any more. Come with us and we will take you to where you will be happy.'

And then you become aware, perhaps in the distance, at the end of a tunnel, of a light. You are drawn towards this light. As you get closer your mind clears. All the darkness and heaviness drops away and suddenly you are free.

This is what happens when spirits are released. They make the transition to the spiritual dimension, to the place where they should have gone immediately after death, the place to which we are all destined to go once we leave the physical world behind. And that is what is meant by 'going into the light'.

Many dimensions

What do we know about the spirit world? Actually, quite a lot, and our knowledge is not based upon faith and speculation. Since Spiritualism began over a hundred and fifty years ago, innumerable accounts have been received, through mediums, from those living in the Beyond.

They tell us that the world beyond death is not somewhere up in the sky. It is not located in physical space at all. It would be more accurate to think of it as another dimension, or perhaps a parallel universe. There are in fact many dimensions or planes. When a person dies – unless for some reason they remain bound to the earth – they enter the first of these dimensions, which Spiritualists call the Summerland. This plane, which I will describe in more detail presently, is only a small step removed from the earthly world.

The process of death

Although it is universally feared and dreaded, the process of death is not something to be afraid of. We have evidence for this not only from spirit communicators but from those who have had near death experiences (NDEs), who have died and been resuscitated by doctors. From such experiences we learn that the dying person slips out of the physical body as easily as if they were discarding an old worn-out overcoat. They feel light and free. There is no fear at all. Next moment, they are standing beside the physical body or else floating in the air a few feet above it.

Most people are met at this point by someone who has come from the spirit world to take care of them. This may be a parent or grandparent, a husband or wife or perhaps a spirit guide. For others, the meeting takes place at a later stage. The death experience is slightly different for every individual.

A very common feature of the NDE is what researchers call the Tunnel. The person has the sensation of travelling at great speed down a long, dark tunnel. Some people perceive it as a valley or a dark void in space. Still there is no fear, but rather a sense of peace and euphoria and being enveloped in love. One account, given in Raymond Moody's book *Life After Life*, reads:

> I had the feeling that I was moving through a deep, dark valley. The darkness was so deep and impenetrable that I could see absolutely nothing but this was the most wonderful, worry-free experience you can imagine.

Another person called it 'a feeling of limbo, of being halfway here and halfway somewhere else'. This is a very apt description because the tunnel represents the passage from the earth to the next dimension. At the end of the tunnel is a light that is dazzlingly bright, yet which does not hurt the eyes. This is the light of the spirit world.

Arriving in the spirit world

Not all spirits have the sensation of travelling through a tunnel. Some simply wake up to find that they have arrived in the spirit world. A friend of mine who died in hospital of cancer communicated with me after her passing saying how frightened she had been of dying despite the fact that she did believe there was a life beyond.

'But I needn't have worried,' she told me, speaking to me telepathically. And she said that she had just drifted off in her sleep. When she woke up she had a shock. She was floating in the air several feet above her body. She looked down at her body in the bed.

'I felt sorry for it,' she said. 'Was that old, frail thing really me?' She saw a nurse bending over her – then suddenly the scene changed. 'I was in a garden,' she went on. 'It was like my grandparents' garden where I used to go as a child. It was so beautiful. Such peace and light – light everywhere. I was dazed. I couldn't take it in at first. But my mother and grandmother were there, holding out their arms to me and I knew I was safe.'

Life in the spirit world

So what is it like, the world that lies beyond? My friend couldn't describe it to me in words but she gave me a visual impression of scenery like the earth but in a more rarified form. Some people who have had NDEs have been given a brief glimpse of this place and describe it in much the same terms. They invariably say that it was so beautiful that they didn't want to return to earth. They speak of a beautiful landscape with trees and flowers and vivid colours that do not exist on earth. The peace and joy are overwhelming and everything is permeated by love.

The surprising thing about this world is that it is so much like the earth. Every region of the earth has its equivalent in the Beyond, so that newly arrived spirits find themselves in surroundings similar to those they have left behind. There are towns and cities as well as countryside. People live in houses, either with family members who have pre-deceased them or, if they were not very fond of their relatives, with other spirits they meet with whom they have an affinity.

Children who die young grow up in the spirit world and are there waiting to greet their parents when they arrive. Animals, too, survive and many people are delighted to be reunited with their much-loved pets. Everything is peace and harmony. There is no pain, hardship or suffering. There is no work of the kind we have here; no offices, shops or factories. There is, however, work of a spiritual kind. There is much to enjoy as many of the things that give us pleasure on earth, such as books, music and art, also exist there.

The spirits who inhabit this plane are not angels. They are ordinary men and women who retain their earthly personalities. Because they are in a higher state of consciousness they are more loving than they were here and wiser, although this does not mean that they are all-knowing. Like us, they are still learning.

As their world is not far away from ours they are able if they wish to revisit the earth, watch over their families and assist them as much as they can by the power of their thoughts. When they come through to their loved ones in sittings, as they are very pleased to do, they bring love and joy with them.

Spirits can remain in the Summerland for as long as they wish, and many do stay there for centuries of our time, although theirs is a timeless state. But they eventually reach a point where they feel the need to leave this environment behind so that they can make further progress. When this happens, they pass from the Summerland to the dimensions beyond. There are many of these dimensions, each more highly evolved than the one before. The higher dimensions are very different from the earth, though what they are like the spirits find hard to describe to us, as they are planes of pure light and energy.

Life in the spirit world is a progression, moving ever forward from one dimension to another as the spirit learns and grows. From time to time, as part of that progression, the spirit returns to earth and incarnates into another body. The subject of reincarnation is one which I do not have space to explore in this book. However, the evidence for it is very strong and it does seem that we all live many times. My understanding is that this earth is a school where we come to learn the lessons and undergo the experiences we need for our soul's growth. Between each life we return to the spirit world, which is our true home.

Eventually, though it may take aeons of time, the spirit reaches a level at which it has learned all the earthly world has to teach. After this, it has no need to return to earth again. From this point on the spirit has little contact with our world unless it chooses to concern itself with the physical plane and to work as a guide, teacher or healer. Those wise beings I call the rescuers come from these higher planes.

Hell and judgement

Many people who have had NDEs describe an experience that has become known as the life review. They say that they saw the whole of their life played out before them in vivid flashbacks. Not only did they witness the scenes but they relived the emotions and, perhaps more significantly, they were aware of the feelings of other people with whom their lives were involved. If they had hurt someone or caused them pain, then during the life review they felt that person's pain within themselves.

This is a profound experience that can bring about great remorse. 'If only I hadn't done that! If only I could take those words back! If only I had been more understanding!' The more the person mistreated others, the more they have to reproach themselves with.

Spirits who have communicated from the spirit world also speak of undergoing some sort of life review. This is the kind of judgement everyone faces after death. But it is undertaken with the help of loving spiritual teachers, and is not a punishment but rather an opportunity for the spirit to assess itself, to consider what faults it needs to correct and what lessons it still has to learn. There is also a sense of satisfaction for things that have been done well and the chance to make progress by giving spiritual service, perhaps to those still on earth.

Spirits are not hauled up before the throne of God to be sentenced and there is no hell of fire and brimstone. That does not mean that cruelty and wickedness go unpunished – but here again, the punishment is a self-imposed one. The spirit world contains planes of darkness as well as planes of light. There is a spiritual law that like attracts like. A spirit whose nature is dark or evil, if it does not remain bound to the earth plane, is automatically drawn towards the darkness.

These dark planes are different from the traditional picture of hell with fire and brimstone. They are hells of the spirit and the mind; dark and depressing as the consciousness of those who inhabit them.

Earthbound spirits who are destructive or full of hatred and malice cannot be allowed to go straight to the Summerland when they are taken away by the rescuers. They are not fitted for it, and the dazzling light would be too bright for them. But neither are they automatically condemned. The rescuers show love to all, recognising that every soul has a spark of divinity within it. If the spirit responds to their love then it can be taken to a place of correction where it is helped to overcome its inner darkness. However, any spirit that deliberately turns away from the light will gravitate towards the regions of darkness.

Yet these hells are not permanent. As soon as the spirit comes to a realisation of its wrongdoing and understands that it is held in darkness only of its own volition, it is free to turn towards the light. At this stage, the rescuers will draw close to bring it love and forgiveness so that it can begin to progress.

The importance of spirituality

This brief and very incomplete picture of the life beyond death is very different from that presented by the church. It indicates that death is not a point at which the fate of the soul is decided for all time. There is no vengeful God sitting on a cloud, sending good people to heaven and consigning sinners to hell for all eternity. To die is simply to take one more step along the soul's journey.

This can be a difficult concept for anyone brought up in the Christian tradition to grasp. There are many Christians who, when they arrive on the other side of life, are quite shocked to find how erroneous their beliefs were. They are shocked, too, to find that they are not the only ones there.

Everyone survives death, whether they want to or not. What we will discover when we get over to the other side of life is that it doesn't matter whether we followed any particular religion or went to church. Nor do fame and money count for anything in the next world. The only thing that will be important is whether we sought to find the light within ourselves and to express that light in the way we lived our lives. The more we do that while we are living here, the happier we will be in the next dimension.

Atheists in the Beyond

For me, as for all those who are aware of the spirit world, it is a great joy to know that death is the beginning of a new phase of existence and that loved ones who have died are not lost to us. I therefore find it hard to understand those determined sceptics who reject all the evidence for the Afterlife because they don't want it to be true. Those who take this attitude still find it hard to believe, even after they are dead!

An interesting account is given in *What Happens When You Die* by Robert Crookall. Dr Karl Novotny, a pupil of the psychologist Alfred Adler, died in 1965. Shortly afterwards, a friend of his went to consult a medium, who transmitted this account from him of what happened when he left the physical body. Novotny told how he had gone for a walk with some friends, despite being ill. Suddenly, during the walk, he was surprised to find that he was feeling well and was no longer tired or out of breath.

I turned back to my companions and found myself looking down at my own body on the ground. My friends were in despair, calling for a doctor, and trying to get a car to take me home. But I was well and felt no pains. I couldn't understand what had happened … When all the formalities had been completed and my body had been put in a coffin, I realised that I must be dead. But I wouldn't acknowledge the fact; for, like my teacher, Alfred Adler, I did not believe in afterlife.

Novotny went to visit a friend in her home but she could not see or hear him. At length he had to recognise the truth.

When finally I did so, I saw my dear mother coming to meet me with open arms, telling me that I had passed into the next world – not in words, of course, since these only belong to the earth. Even so, I couldn't credit her statement and thought I must be dreaming. This belief continued for a long time. I fought against the truth and was most unhappy.

Why more people don't become earthbound

In the materialistic society in which we live today there are a great many who have no religious faith and no belief in any kind of existence beyond death. You might expect, therefore, that a lot of people would become earthbound when they die. But this is not the case. Fortunately, not many are such determined atheists as Novotny. As soon as they find themselves free of the body yet still very much alive, they are obliged to admit that there is life after death – and most of them are quite happy about it.

We are essentially spiritual beings. We lose sight of this fact while we are in the physical world but the knowledge is still there in the inner self. As soon as the body is left behind the spirit comes into its own. It returns to its own element, back into the light. And because this is the dimension it came from before the earth life, it finds the place familiar.

The spirit is like a balloon. While it is in the physical body it is tethered to the physical world. As soon as the body dies, the tie is cut and the 'balloon' automatically ascends. This will always happen – unless there is something that holds it down, as a balloon might be held down by a piece of string that becomes entangled around some obstacle. The 'piece of string' may be emotional pain or trauma, attachment to material things, habit or any of the causes that render a spirit earthbound. As the spirit is released the 'string' is disentangled and then there is nothing to prevent it from returning home.

The strongest ties that hold a spirit earthbound are those that exist with loved ones left behind. The ability to stay in touch after death is, in most cases, a great source of comfort and consolation to those on both sides of life. But sometimes the strength of that love and the pain associated with the passing can be so great that the spirit is held back and cannot progress.

8
Ties That Bind

Karen Browne was lying snug and warm in bed when suddenly she woke up from a deep sleep to see her grandfather standing by her side.

> He was smiling at me and his gaze was radiating pure love. Then he spoke using his pet name for me, saying, 'I'm going away now, my wee dove.' I smiled back at him and lay back down to sleep, pausing only to look at the clock before closing my eyes. The time was 6 am.

Karen's grandparents lived in a ground floor flat below her and her parents and the whole family were very close. Strangely, it didn't occur to her to question why her grandfather should have been standing by her bed at six in the morning. Shortly afterwards, she was woken by the sound of her grandmother screaming. Her grandfather had died in bed. Everyone was in shock, yet Karen felt strangely calm and comforted by the fact that he had come to say goodbye to her. Later, when she read the death certificate, she learned that he had died of a heart attack, which the doctor estimated to have happened at 6 am.

Contact soon after death

This story, given in *After-Death Communication* by Emma Heathcote-James, is typical of the innumerable accounts that have been reported of spirits appearing at the time of their death or very shortly afterwards. So common is this phenomenon that parapsychologists have given it a name – crisis apparitions. As in Karen's case, often the person who sees the apparition does not know at that time that the person is dead.

When a person realises that they have passed out of the physical world, their first thought is usually for those they have left behind. They are anxious that the survivors will be shocked and grieving and this concern immediately draws them back to the people they are worried about. Because of the intensity of the spirit's emotions they are able to break through the veil that normally separates the earth from the spirit world. That is why, following a death, those who have been bereaved frequently say that they feel as if the person who has died is still around. Even people who wouldn't normally consider themselves to be psychic have psychic experiences at these times. They may catch a glimpse of the spirit, usually out of the corner of the eye, or notice a characteristic smell such as a perfume or cigarettes. They may even hear noises or notice that small objects have been moved.

These things can lead them to believe that they have a haunting, much to the dismay of the spirit, who doesn't want to frighten them but just wants to let them know that he is there. Imagine dying and coming back to your family home and seeing your relatives grieving for you, even arranging your funeral. You long to speak to them, to tell them that you are alive, but you can't get through. You talk to them but they don't hear. You stand in front of them, jumping up and down and waving your arms around but they take no notice. Maybe, giving vent to your frustration, you knock over an ornament or slam a door. This only frightens them more and they assume that you are a ghost, and call in the vicar to exorcise you!

Trying to get through

Spirits make great efforts to get through to those they love. If the survivor understands about life after death and accepts that they are there in their spirit form, even if they cannot actually see them or speak to them, this helps the spirit to be at peace and makes it easier for them to come to terms with their transition. When the survivor sends out a powerful thought – 'please let me know that you are safe!' they will do their best to get that reassurance across.

Here is another example from Emma Heathcote-James's book. Heather Davies suffered a terrible shock when her husband died suddenly while they were out having a meal together:

> I kept saying that, if only I knew he was safe, I could pick up the pieces and carry on. I just wanted to know he was all right.

8/8/2
19 70

E Kelly Gentry

Essex

to Blake Avenue

Barking

Love you dad
"always"

Dad I Love you
with all of my
heart & soul
I'm so sorry
I miss you so
much
I'm not asking
you to forgive me
please don't hate
me
I love you dad
♡ x x x x x x

that relationship I
was in he beat me
up all the time he
raped me he
finished me in
everyway he
would get angry
if i danced with
you or got close
as my dad i
would get hit again
again again again

You was always
an amazing dad
I let you down
So much you
never brought
me up to be
like I don't know
what happened
to me
The only thing I
think off is

One night, when she was unable to sleep, she summoned up every ounce of psychic energy she could muster and called out to him in her mind.

It was instant. The room lit up – part ceiling and part top of the wall. The rest of the room was in darkness and the edge between the two swirly mist. It was an upright oblong with the edges rounded. There was the most beautiful man in white robes, holy and saintly, and he said in a lovely voice, 'He wants to speak to you,' and he glided to one side and the last thing I saw of him was the cuff of his sleeve, which was pointed. As he glided to one side there was my husband stood behind him looking really well, not dreadful as he had been looking in the ambulance on that dreaded night, but really rested and well. I felt I hadn't got long and said, 'Derek, are you all right?' and he said to me reassuringly, 'I'm all right,' then it was all gone.

I felt enormously privileged. I was then able to sleep and slowly I rebuilt my life. I felt that my husband had asked for permission to come and put my mind at ease. I don't think he could go on until then. I felt that he was going on a journey.

Spirits sometimes find it possible to get through to their loved ones during their sleep. The survivor will experience vivid dreams in which they recall meeting the person they love. These are in fact more than dreams. When we go to sleep at night the spirit self leaves the physical body and, in that state, we can be with those in the spirit dimension. Once again, however, the poor spirit is frustrated when the person fails to remember anything about it in the morning or dismisses it with, 'It was only a dream!'

I have known many instances where a spirit, unable to

reach the person to whom they wanted to speak, has tried to contact a third party to ask them to pass on some message. My sitters are often surprised to hear from someone they didn't know, or with whom they were only distantly connected, and to receive a request to convey some words of comfort and consolation to the spirit's family on earth.

Some spirits wait around for a long time, hoping that, in some way or other, they can get through to those they care about. If they are never acknowledged they eventually give up and go away but they are sad to leave without having had the opportunity to communicate.

Is my loved one earthbound?

In the days and weeks following their passing the spirit is going through a period of adjustment. Like a climber acclimatising themselves to a higher altitude they have to acclimatise themselves to their spiritual state. During this period, although they have gone into the light, they spend much time revisiting their homes and families. The period of adjustment may be short or may last months or even years. It depends upon the spirit's attachment to the earth and their loved ones, and upon the degree to which the surviving family members need them to stay close.

Maureen came to see me because she was worried about her husband Ron, who had died some months before. 'I've always believed in life after death,' she told me. 'After Ron died, I knew he was with me. At times I almost felt as if I could reach out and touch him.'

I asked her if she was frightened by this. On the contrary,

she told me, she was glad to have him there. But as time went on she felt that he was still just as close as he had been immediately after his passing and she was concerned. 'Shouldn't he have moved on by now?' she asked. 'Does this mean he's earthbound?'

I assured her that this wasn't the case. Tuning in to Ron, I could feel that there was a light and vibrancy about him which would not have been there had he been earthbound. But he was remaining close to his wife's side because she needed him so much. He asked me, 'How could I go on and leave her like this?'

Maureen understood why he should feel this way. She and Ron had been married for over fifty years. Even with the knowledge she had of life after death she was finding it extremely hard to cope with his passing.

A few months later, she came to see me again. This time she looked brighter, but now she had another anxiety.

'He's still around,' she told me, 'but he feels different. Not quite so close, somehow. Does this mean he's going away?'

Once again, I reassured her. 'He loves you too much for that. All that's happened is that he's moved on a bit. I expect that's because you're coping better now?'

Maureen admitted that this was true. Although she still missed him terribly, she was gradually getting her life back together again. But I knew that Ron would never be far from her side.

Till death do us part

Where there is a deep bond of love between two people it is never broken, even by death. The vow is made 'till death do us part', but in fact death does not part those who are closely united. The person who has died continues to look after and care for the survivor. This, however, does not make them earthbound. They are staying close of their own accord.

To explain what happens and why, let's take Ron's case as an example. Ron died after a long illness, during which Maureen nursed him devotedly. When he died he was met by his parents. With them beside him, he passed into the light. But his thoughts were still with Maureen and how she was suffering. These strong thoughts drew him back to her. He was glad that she could sense he was there, and he did all he could to make her aware of his presence in order to bring her comfort.

At that time, Maureen was able to sense him in an almost tangible way. But as time went on and she began to come to terms with her loss, he started to detach himself from the earth plane. Maureen perceived this as a moving away. Of course, he hadn't forgotten about her or ceased to care for her. He had simply moved on a little, adjusted more to the spirit dimension. He was therefore on a slightly higher vibration, so Maureen couldn't feel his presence in such a physical way. The higher the rate of vibration on which spirits exist, the harder it is for those on earth to be aware of them.

The close companionship between this loving couple would continue until it was time for Maureen to pass over. But instead of hovering around her all the time, Ron was dividing his time between her and his new home in the spirit world. The situation was better for both of them. It meant that he could enter fully into his new life and, at the same time, she could get on with her life. But he was never going to move so far away that he was beyond her reach. He was still sensitive to the thoughts and the love she was sending out to him and could be at her side immediately, at any time she needed him.

Sorting out practical problems

When a person dies they often leave behind many practical issues to be sorted out. This is especially difficult when, as in Maureen's case, the surviving partner is left alone after many years of companionship. As well as coping with their grief they have to make difficult decisions. 'What should I do with his things?' 'Will he mind if I give his clothes to a charity shop?' 'Should I sell the house and move to somewhere smaller?' They want to carry out the deceased person's wishes but, if the person left no instructions, they cannot be sure what they would have wanted.

Their loved one in spirit is aware of all this but, if the survivor has no sense that the loved one is present, it will be powerless to do anything to help. If, however, the survivor is receptive the spirit may be able to drop information or suggestions into their mind as to how to handle these difficult issues.

Very common concerns at these times are, 'What sort of funeral would he like?' or 'Where should I scatter the ashes?' Spirits are seldom bothered by these matters. They often attend their own funeral and appreciate the care taken over the service. They are aware of what the mourners are thinking and feeling and, if the expressions of grief are not sincere, they will know about it! But they are not usually worried over what happens to their physical remains. Their concern is only to see their loved ones through this painful time.

At a sitting I gave recently, a husband in spirit communicating with his wife told her how upset he was at the squabble that had broken out in the family about the money he had left. He said that he was happy for her to distribute it among the family members in any way she wished, but advised her to keep a sizeable chunk for herself – and have a good time with it!

However, those left behind can be quite cold-hearted in their attitude towards the dear departed. One husband who came through to his wife had been a deep thinker when on earth, interested in the subject of life after death but not fully convinced. 'He's saying that he's found the answer to his questions,' I began. 'And he wants you to know that the spirit world –'

'Yes, yes,' she interrupted impatiently. 'Never mind all that. I want to know where he's left his will!'

Held back by grief

It is only natural to grieve for the death of a loved one but there are situations where that grief is so deep, and where the mourner holds on to it so tightly, that it hinders the spirit from moving forward. Some spirits are caught up in the survivor's emotional turmoil. Although they desperately try to bring comfort, their efforts only make it worse for the survivor, who subconsciously picks up and carries the spirit's pain as well as their own.

This is most likely to happen in situations where the person who died had no spiritual understanding and no belief in anything beyond death. Such spirits cling to their earthly loved one because they want more than anything else to remain with them. In fact, these spirits may not realise that there is anywhere else to go. Either they do not see the light because of the dark clouds around the person on earth, or they do see it but are unwilling to enter it. They do not understand that, if they go into the light, they can then return to visit their loved one – and that, in doing so, they can be of much more help because they can then share the light and strength that they themselves will have found.

Those who had spiritual awareness rarely become stuck in this way. Such spirits feel deeply for the survivor's grief and, as I have said elsewhere, they may choose to spend much of their time close to those they have left behind. But they have reached a level of consciousness where they understand that the separation is only temporary and that they will one day be reunited with those they love.

Marilyn lost her only son in a tragic accident. Devastated, she buried herself in grief, shutting out her husband and her daughters who were trying to console her. Her only comfort was in the belief that, somehow, she might be able to contact him. She turned his room into a shrine. Day after day, she shut herself away in there, willing him to appear or to speak to her.

Eventually, after weeks of trying, she had a vivid dream in which he appeared. He spoke to her with great love, telling her that all was well. But he added, 'Please, Mum, let me go. I can't move on while you are so unhappy.'

Fortunately, she accepted this dream as a real meeting with him and took the lesson to heart. She set him free and started living again.

Helping a loved one who has died

Marilyn's reaction was understandable. There is, perhaps, no greater tragedy that can befall anyone than losing a child. But whatever our relationship to the person who has died, we need to express grief at times of loss, otherwise we can never heal the hurt. Those in the spirit world are well aware of this need. Even when they have passed into the light, they miss us as we miss them, although they do have the consolation of being in a beautiful world.

However, there is much that you can do at times like this, to help yourself through the period of mourning. Should your loved one be having difficulty in moving on, you can help them as well.

+ Send out loving thoughts to the person who has died. If you feel their presence, acknowledge to them, either aloud or in your mind, that you know they are there.
+ Don't be frightened by anything that happens, such as the sense of being touched, by smells or by moving objects. It is just their way of letting you know they are around.
+ Speak to them about your feelings. Don't try to hold back the tears.
+ If there is anything you want to ask them, ask the questions then listen quietly. You may hear the reply in your mind, or sense whatever they are trying to tell you. This may not happen immediately, but often the answer will drop into your mind at some later time when you are relaxed and not thinking about anything in particular.
+ Make the funeral a celebration of the person's life. If you want to place flowers in the cemetery or garden of

remembrance, by all means do so as they will know about it and appreciate the love. But it is even better to put the flowers in your home where you – and they – can see and enjoy them.

✦ You may wish to go and see a medium, in order to make a clearer, more direct contact with your loved one. (See Resources for information about finding a medium.) It is thought by some people that spirits are not able to communicate until some time after their death and that the bereaved should wait for several weeks before having a sitting. In my experience, I have not found this to be true. The period immediately after their passing is the time when they feel the strongest need to get through. I would therefore advise that you book a sitting as soon as you wish.

As time gradually begins to heal the wounds, start living your own life again. You will never lose your loved one by doing this. In fact, the more they see you happy, the happier and more at peace they will be!

Held back by negative emotions

The ties that bind spirits to those on earth are not always ties of love. Negative emotions such as remorse, jealousy and hatred can also hold a spirit back.

Laura, a medium I once knew, was divorced from her husband. Some years later she met a charming widower and they wanted to get married, but the man's dead wife had other ideas. Being a medium does occasionally have disadvantages. Mediums learn to close down their psychic senses to the spirit world when they want to, but in Laura's case, she found herself unable to shut out the jealous wife, who had a strong, determined mind, and would insist upon intruding at their most intimate moments.

This is, I hasten to explain, an unusual situation. In every other instance I have come across, the partner in spirit has been glad for the survivor to find happiness again, only expressing concern if they think they have chosen someone who will not be good for them. But spirits who are earthbound, as this one was, still feel the same emotions they would have done on earth. Laura tried to move her on but she refused to go. Eventually, Laura gave up the struggle and called off the engagement.

When someone dies with a mind full of hatred or resentment, they carry this emotion over with them and it prevents them from entering into the light. They are tied to the person for whom they harboured such bad feelings and can have a destructive influence upon their lives.

To say that Pat, a client I saw a few years ago, had a difficult relationship with her mother-in-law Vera would be an understatement. Vera believed that her beloved son had married beneath him and did all she could to undermine their relationship. When Vera became ill, Pat swallowed her dislike and visited her every day, attending to her every need, but she received no thanks for it. In fact, the more Vera became dependent on her daughter-in-law, the more she seemed to hate her.

Eventually Vera died. Pat breathed a sigh of relief, thinking that her problems were at an end. But her mother-in-law's malice pursued her from beyond the grave. Pat began having bad dreams in which Vera appeared. She found herself in the grip of a depression she couldn't shake off. She even experienced physical symptoms similar to those Vera had suffered. It took a great deal of persuasion to deal with Vera. The guides eventually moved her on – but I wasn't entirely convinced that she had gone for good.

Another client, Joan, came to see me because she felt stuck in her life. She had suffered a run of bad luck which included being made redundant and finding herself unable to get another job. She was also very depressed.

The spirit I picked up with Joan was her father. I knew that he, like her, was stuck and I wasn't surprised when she told me that her depression and her other problems had started six months before, just after her father died.

Joan and her father had never got on. Towards the end of his life there had been a partial reconciliation but there was still bad feeling between them. Because of this, he had cut her out of his will, leaving all his money to another relative who, as Joan said, already had plenty of money and didn't need it, whereas she was in real financial difficulties.

What emanated from her father when he came through to me was a mixture of anger and remorse. He had never forgiven Joan for what he saw as her failure to understand him, yet now that he was in the spirit world he saw things more clearly. He was deeply sorry that he had not provided for her and, at the same time, frustrated that there was nothing he could do to put things right.

I explained this to Joan, who completely forgave him. This released her father to go into the light. From that time on, her depression lifted and her life took a turn for the better.

The importance of forgiveness

Remorse can be a strong factor in holding spirits earthbound. From their new vantage point they see the pain they have caused but it is too late to do anything about it. They need the forgiveness of those on earth in order to be able to progress to the level of understanding where they are able to forgive themselves and let go of guilt and blame.

But those left behind have to forgive for their own sakes too. Joan's anger towards her father was binding him to her and causing her to be stuck in her existence just as he was stuck in his. In the case of Pat and her mother-in-law, the bond of hatred that had built up between them had continued beyond death. Both were caught up in it and neither could break the link. I lost touch with Pat soon after her visit to me so I do not know if the problem was ever resolved. But I hope that they found it in their hearts to forgive each other, so that both of them could be set free.

Sometimes, with the best will in the world, we cannot bring ourselves to love or even like those relatives or associates with whom our lives are interwoven. The teaching of the spirit world is that we are brought into contact with such people to teach us tolerance, patience and understanding. I cannot help thinking that it is one thing to acknowledge this intuitively and quite another to put it into practice when we are confronted with a difficult in-law, an overbearing parent or a problem child! But we have to try to see beyond the human personality and realise that every person upon this earth is in essence a spirit being, struggling along their own pathway and coping in the only way they know how. Perhaps at some time they have been wounded or have never been shown love. For ultimately it is love that enables us all to rise beyond the earthly level of consciousness and find our way home to the spirit world.

Never is love and forgiveness more necessary than in cases where, for whatever reason, a person has been driven to take their own life.

9

Suicide

Suicide is a desperate last resort when life seems hopeless or pointless. But when a person who has taken their own life arrives in the spirit world, they are often overwhelmed with regret and full of remorse when they see the effect of their action on those who love them.

In the past the church taught that suicide was a mortal sin. It was believed that those who had committed suicide were condemned to wander in limbo until such time as their allotted lifespan ended. Even today, when attitudes have become more liberal and tolerant, many writers on the subject state dogmatically that those who commit suicide always become earthbound. In my long experience of working with spirit communicators, I have not found this to be the case. Suicide is, of course, never a positive option and it does impede the spirit's progress in the Beyond, but it does not necessarily make the spirit earthbound. As ever, there are no hard and fast rules.

The importance of motive

One person might decide to end their life because they are suffering a terminal illness and are no longer able to endure the pain. Another might do so when they are in a deep depression. Someone with a strong sense of honour might see it as the only way out of a situation in which they were no longer able to face themselves or the world. These are very different motives. Outsiders might consider that such actions were wrong and misguided. It is only in the spirit world that each soul's innermost feelings are fully under-stood. Only the spirit guides, and the spirit themselves, can judge and decide whether or not what they did was justified.

Those spirits who suffer the most seem to be those who killed themselves as a form of escape from situations or problems they did not have the courage to deal with, or perhaps as an act of spite towards someone they wanted to hurt. Too late, they find that they have hurt themselves most of all. They see that they have wasted their God-given opportunities and devastated the lives of their families. Such spirits often find it difficult to communicate. Their bitter regret sets up a barrier that is hard for them to break through. When they do get through they lament, 'If only I could put back the clock and start again!'

I would, however, say two things, for the benefit of readers who may have lost a loved one in this tragic way. The first is that suicides are never condemned by the spirit world. Whatever their motives, they are treated with great love and compassion. Any suffering they undergo is a result of their self-recrimination; it is not because they are being punished.

In this life, if someone attempts suicide but fails, they are, hopefully, helped rather than judged. They may be given counselling or therapy to help them overcome their emotional problems. It is similar in the spirit world. Such spirits receive healing and understanding, enabling them to view their lives from a higher perspective. In this way they learn the deep underlying causes for their actions and are shown to how sort themselves out.

While there may be little they can do to put things right on earth (though they can be with their families spiritually), they discover that there are ways in which they can make amends. Sometimes they work in the spirit dimension, helping other people who are in despair or who have also died by their own hand.

The second thing I would say is that it is of immense help to such spirits if they are able to get in touch with those on earth for whom they are concerned. When a person commits suicide their family is often left with a deep sense of guilt. They wonder whether there were any warning signs they should have spotted or if there was anything they could have done to prevent it. If there was no apparent motive for the suicide, they torment themselves with questions as to why it happened. The person in spirit needs to explain. They need to say how sorry they are, to offer comfort and seek forgiveness. When they can do this, it lightens their burden and helps them to move forward.

Peter's story

Peter was a bright, intelligent young man nearing the end of his university career. He had a lovely girlfriend and they had just set up home together. He seemed to have everything to live for. But there was a shadow hanging over him. All his life he had suffered from depression, and it had become increasingly severe over the years, despite constant medication. However, he was doing his utmost to fight against it and it seemed to his parents, Sheila and Bill, that at last he was succeeding. Then Peter and his girlfriend had a row which culminated in her walking out. It was the last straw. That night, he took an overdose of sleeping pills. A friend found him in the morning and phoned his parents.

I need hardly say that Sheila and Bill were devastated. But they had one comfort. They understood that there was life after death, and Sheila especially felt that Peter was around. However, she was worried that he was not at peace. They came to me for a sitting and as I felt Peter draw close to me I found my eyes filling with tears. His emotion was overpowering.

'I'm so sorry,' he said over and over again. 'I was so depressed. I just couldn't fight against it any more.'

He explained that it had been an impulsive action. All he could think of on that fatal night was how low he was feeling. Not even the knowledge of what it would do to his parents had been enough to stop him. He explained that his grandmother had met him and taken him to a place of healing. He had not been blamed for what he had done. He was not, and never had been, in darkness. In fact, his mind was clearer than ever. The depression had been an illness over which he had no control. Had he failed in that attempt, he realised, he would have got worse and worse and at some time he would have tried again.

He told his parents how much he loved them and that he would always be with them. This contact brought peace to him and to them. They had a difficult time ahead, but for Peter, while he was aware of their sorrow, the pathway was now open to a fuller, happier life.

The bishop's son

I have encountered all too many cases similar to this. Many souls coming to our world today are highly sensitive and spiritually aware. Like Peter, they find it hard to deal with the harsh realities of this world, its cruelty and injustice, and often feel like outsiders among their less sensitive peers. Their inability to cope may lead them to depression or dependency on drugs or alcohol, sometimes with tragic consequences.

The story of another young man who took his own life is told in *The Other Side* by James A. Pike. This book, published in 1969, gives a clear insight into what happens after death to those who pass in such circumstances. Pike, Bishop of California, was a controversial clergyman who at one time was charged with heresy. He caused even more of a stir when, following the death of his son, he made public this account of his contact with him after death.

Jim Pike committed suicide through a drug overdose. Immediately afterwards, his father experienced psychic activity in the flat he and his son had shared. Objects disappeared and turned up again in unlikely places. Clothes in the wardrobe were pulled off their hangers and flung around in disarray. A clock stopped with its hands pointing at 8.19 – the exact time of Jim's death.

With an open-mindedness that would have shocked his ecclesiastical colleagues, the bishop went for a sitting with

Ena Twigg, a leading medium of the day. Jim made contact at once and it was clear from the medium's reaction as Jim drew close to her that he was in some distress. Speaking through the medium, he explained that he hadn't known what he was doing at the time he took his life, and added:

I'm tied to my regrets. Yet they are showing me the way out and we must make progress together ... This is the way to freedom: to come back and try to explain ... I've been so unhappy because I didn't have a voice and had to find a way to tell you. I thought there was a way out; I wanted out; I've found there is no way out. I wish I'd stayed to work out my problems in more familiar surroundings.

In a later sitting he spoke at greater length:

You know I came over here in a state of great mental confusion and – not antagonism towards the world, but in a state of not understanding and being afraid to trust people. You knew that. And I had to come to terms with the situation, and when I came over here they said, 'Now, come along. Academic qualifications won't help you here. Let's get down to the basics'; and we tried to find out what are the things that really matter – to have compassion and understanding and to be kind ... And gradually I began to get a sense of pattern, you know. I began to find that this was one way of release. This was religion, without somebody forcing God and Jesus down my throat. And I find that by working this way I could find a philosophy that religion hadn't been able to give me ... I thought, if they all come to me, all the blessed saints, all come trooping in, I'll have none of it. I couldn't accept it on those terms. And I didn't think they would want me to because they knew me, didn't they? Those invisible people knew me. So they cater for the individual need and lead you, so gently, so kindly. They show you things that are essential and they put the things that are not essential on one side.

So I gradually began to get a sense of belonging again. And one great thing that was a stimulus and a great help was to know that I have got this one foot on earth and I could reach you ... And that's what I wanted to say to the family; I am all right, don't worry.

He spoke of the new world he had entered as an exciting place where all was peace and harmony and where he felt more alive than he ever had on earth.

Jim had found his way into the light and was making progress. He was basically a spiritually orientated young man and this helped him to adjust to life in a spiritual dimension. For those who do not have such knowledge when they are alive and whose lives are similarly cut short, the transition can be harder. It takes them longer to find peace.

Alcohol and drug abuse

For many people today drug taking is an accepted way of life. Some view it as a harmless recreation and are able to control their use of such substances, but others slip all too easily into addiction. Those who die as a result of alcohol or drug abuse have to bear a heavy burden of guilt because they have thrown their life away. Because the drugs have affected their mind, they are in a state of confusion when they arrive on the other side, and this makes it more difficult for them to sort out their problems.

Simon, like Peter, was a university student with a promising career before him. He took drugs occasionally, as did many of his friends, but thought he had it well under control. Then one night at a party he accidentally took one dose too many – and woke up in the spirit world.

Because Simon wasn't an addict, he woke up with a clear head. But when he came through to me in a sitting I did for his father, he was weeping with remorse. 'How could I have been so stupid?' he asked. 'I'm so sorry – what a waste!'

Making contact with his family and knowing that they forgave him did help him. But, despite the love he had received in the spirit dimension, I felt that he would carry his remorse for a very long time.

Melanie

Many of those who take their own lives are never able to make any contact with their families. For them, it is harder to come to terms with what they have done, while their families never have the comfort of knowing that their son or daughter has survived death.

In their desperation to get through to someone on earth, they may hover around any sensitive person they can find. That person may then become depressed or find themselves behaving in ways that are out of character. This can continue indefinitely, unless they realise what is happening to them.

Sarah Phipps, who wrote to me while I was collecting material for this book, had a young friend called Melanie who sometimes used to babysit for her. One evening while on her way to work she saw Melanie standing outside her house. Psychically, Sarah sensed a black cloud hanging over Melanie's head. A few weeks later, she learned that Melanie had committed suicide. She told me:

'The shock and the rollercoaster of emotions I felt was overwhelming. For weeks I noticed that wherever I went a certain song would be playing on the radio. I couldn't help thinking that maybe it was Melanie's doing, trying to get a message across. As the months went by I started to become obsessed with Melanie's suicide, feeling depressed, crying for no apparent reason, feeling drained and tired. At times I thought I was going mad or heading for a nervous breakdown. I felt as if I'd taken on Melanie's feelings and emotions. I had to make sure Melanie was all right and in a safe place.'

Sarah went to several mediums but received no communication from Melanie. Her mental state was such that she was beginning to contemplate suicide herself.

'One night after a really emotional day I woke up and couldn't take it any more. I was feeling desperate, crying. I begged and prayed that someone or something would help Melanie and me. Then – I can't explain it – it was like a sudden loud crack of lightning in my bedroom. Then everything disappeared. I felt normal and, most important, I felt that Melanie was all right, as if she was now at peace. It was just like a light being switched on.'

What Sarah had sensed was the moment at which Melanie was released, thanks to her prayers. A few months later, Melanie's mother came to Sarah's door. The mother had been to see a medium and had received a message from her daughter saying to send Sarah her love. Sarah was delighted to think that she had been able to help Melanie find peace – but it had taken 18 agonising months.

How to help someone who has taken their own life

Many sitters who come to me after a loved one has taken their own life are consumed with anxiety for them. They want to know if the person is suffering or if they have become earthbound because of what they have done. As the examples in this chapter have shown, victims of suicide are often greatly in need of help, but this does not mean that they are necessarily earthbound. As with any other kinds of passing, it depends upon the individual and their spiritual understanding, or lack of it.

If someone in your family has passed in this tragic way, there is much you can do to help them:

✦ Send out your loving thoughts. Hold their image in your mind and keep projecting love and light towards them.
✦ If you feel that they are around you, talk to them, either in your mind or aloud if you prefer. Try to sense what they are feeling.
✦ Go to see a medium so that, hopefully, you can get in touch. This gives them the opportunity to explain. Bear in mind that suicides do sometimes find it hard to communicate, so be patient. If the first medium you go to see cannot get through to them, try someone else.

Perhaps there is someone you may know of who has committed suicide, but whom you did not know well. If so, you can still help them by sending light and loving thoughts. These always reach the person for whom they are intended.

Sending out such thoughts may draw the person to you. Be aware that this can happen. Should you start to feel depressed, as Sarah did, know that you are picking up the spirit's feelings. It is important that you do not hold on to these feelings. Once again, the best course of action is to see a medium.

If contact is made, and the spirit asks you to pass on a message to their family, try to do so if at all possible. It can take a lot of courage to approach people who, perhaps, you do not know well and whose religious beliefs you are not sure of, in order to tell them that their loved one has been in touch with you. But, if you can bring yourself to do this, you will be giving immense help to the one who has died, as well as helping those closest to them to understand what has happened.

Above all, remember that no one who goes into the spirit world is judged or condemned. Whatever their motive, the suicide victim will have been met with love and understanding. Even if, because of their troubled state of mind, they are having difficulty in finding their way to the light, with your love and prayers you can open the door for them, so that they can enter the beautiful world where they will be at peace.

10
Sudden and Violent Death

The Litany of the Anglican *Book of Common Prayer* contains the petition: 'From battle, murder and from sudden death, Good Lord, deliver us.' The writer of this prayer, though steeped in Christian theology, may have had an intuitive sense that sudden or violent death can cause much suffering for the spirit. In fact, it is one of the main reasons why a spirit may become earthbound. This does not happen in every case, however. As always, it depends upon the individual and the state of their mind at the time of death.

No time to say goodbye

A stroke or heart attack is a very common cause of death, so it is not surprising that many sitters who come to me have lost a relative or friend in this way. The shock of such a loss can be devastating. There is no time to prepare or to say goodbye. Often, there are many issues left unresolved, many words unspoken.

What the mourner fails to realise is that the person who has died may well be feeling the same shock as they are and will be left with the same regrets. As many of the accounts quoted in this book have demonstrated, there is no pain associated with the process of death, but the mind and personality remain just the same as in life. Most spirits feel the need to get in touch with their families, to let them know that they have survived.

This urgent need to communicate is easy to understand. If you were to be plucked, with no warning, from everyone you held dear and transported to a foreign country, wouldn't you want to get in touch with those you had left, to let them know where you were? So it is with spirits. They hover around the survivors, waiting for a chance to get through. If they cannot do this they have to endure the mental agony of watching the survivors struggling with their emotions, and perhaps also with feelings of guilt and regret. It has been truly said that the worst hell is seeing your family grieving – and not being able to do anything to comfort them.

'If only I'd known!'

When Hazel came to see me she was tormenting herself with guilt. Her partner, Mike, who had been in his twenties, had collapsed at work and died of a massive heart attack. He had experienced no previous symptoms of heart trouble so his death was a total shock.

In tears, Hazel confided to me, 'We'd had a terrible row

that morning. I threatened to walk out on him. If only I'd known!'

Tuning in to Mike, I could feel his distress. He was not alone, nor was he in a state of confusion. His mother was with him, surrounding him with love. But all he could think of was Hazel. There was something he desperately needed to say to her. 'He's saying he forgives you,' I told her.

Hazel burst into tears and admitted shamefully, 'I told him that morning I wished he'd drop dead. Those were the last words I said to him. He went out and slammed the door and got into the car and drove off. And I never saw him again.'

I could feel that Mike wanted to throw his arms around her and comfort her. 'He knows that you didn't mean it and he wants you to stop blaming yourself. You both said things you didn't mean. He loves you so much.'

Hazel smiled through her tears with relief. 'As long as he knows that. That makes me feel a bit better.'

There was another reason why Mike wasn't ready to move on. 'He's talking about the baby,' I said.

Hazel told me that she was pregnant and sobbed, 'He'll never see his child grow up.'

'He will,' I told her. 'He'll be watching over you both from the spirit world.'

These words were some consolation to her, but she asked, 'Why did it have to happen? He was so young. He had so much to live for.'

I have been asked that question so many times, by those who lose young people or children, and it is always hard for me to know what to say to comfort them. We are told from the spirit world that, however it may appear from our earthly perspective, every person's passing takes place at the right time, according to what that soul is learning in its eternal path of progress. I know that many people find this teaching impossible to accept and I do not think we will ever find the answers to these difficult questions until we ourselves pass into the spirit world. But I do believe that everything has a purpose and that one day, beyond this life, it will all become clear.

Hazel, however, was not ready to view it like that – and neither was Mike. He was angry that his life had been taken away. He didn't want to be in the spirit dimension. His thoughts were still tied to the earth, to Hazel, to their unborn child, and to his father, who was also in deep grief. He knew that the light was there for him to enter – but he had turned his back on it. He was clinging to Hazel.

I spoke to the pair, telling them that they must both let go. Mike had to move forward into the light, because only then, on a higher level of understanding, would he be able to come to terms with his passing. Hazel had to be willing to let him take that step. The spiritual bond between them would not be broken and the contact would not be lost. But until he entered the light, neither of them would be at peace.

Death in an accident

When someone is seriously injured in an accident and loses consciousness they are dazed and traumatised when they come round. For a while they are likely to be in a state of shock, unable to comprehend what has happened. A person who is killed in an accident suffers the same sort of trauma. They are thrown out of the physical body so abruptly that they are plunged into a state of total shock and disbelief.

What is it like to die in such a way? We have a lot of information about this, both from spirit communications and from near death experiences. What follows is a typical scenario.

A man is driving along the road. He sees another car coming towards him. He realises that they are going to collide and hurriedly swerves, but it is too late. There is a moment's panic, a crash, then nothing. What seems like seconds later, he opens his eyes. He finds himself standing beside the wreckage of the car. He finds that he is uninjured and has no pain – in fact, he feels amazingly vibrant and alive. Puzzled, he concludes that, by some miracle, he has been thrown clear.

He sees the driver of the other car peering anxiously into the wreckage. There is a body in there but the accident victim cannot understand whose body it is. He goes closer to look. The crumpled form bent over the steering wheel looks like him. It *is* him! But how can it be? He is alive!

While he is trying to work it out he sees other motorists who have stopped and are hurrying towards the scene of the accident. He tries to talk to them, to tell them that he is all right, but they take no notice. In fact, they walk straight through him. Slowly, the terrible truth begins to dawn that he has been killed.

So what happens next? This varies from one person to another. For everyone who passes over, whatever the manner of their passing, there is someone to greet them. Those in the spirit world know in advance when the passing is going to occur, so they are there waiting. Generally, the period of confusion is short. Such spirits may not be very pleased to find themselves on the other side, but the person who meets them will explain to them what has happened and will look after them, leading them away from the scene of the accident into the light.

A man who was killed while riding his bicycle told me, 'When it first happened everything was dark. I was in a complete panic.'

Then something wonderful happened. He went on, 'It was as if the whole sky just lit up. I saw my grandparents coming towards me.' And he wanted me to tell his mother, 'Don't keep going over and over it in your mind. I've forgotten it, like forgetting a bad dream. I'm so happy now.'

The story of Philip

Philip, a young man who was killed in a motorcycle accident, communicated with his mother soon after his passing by a technique called automatic writing, in which the spirit writes through the hand of a medium. His mother, Alice Gilbert, later published the account in *Philip in Two Worlds*. Philip described riding very fast down a slope, then there was a crash followed by blackness. He opened his eyes and was surprised to find that he had no bruises.

> Then I saw a car coming, and I jumped up to get out of its way, and I saw it brake, pull up and push something along the road. I looked and it was my body. I looked at myself and saw my own body looking quite real and solid, but there were streams of light coming from my finger ends. Suddenly I saw Grandpa, standing smiling, all lit up and I knew I was killed.

Philip felt muddled and confused but his first impulse was to get back to his mother.

I began walking along the road and got to the door at last, and felt for my key, but it was not there. So I rang the door-bell, but I felt the sound of it, inside me. You opened the window and called but you did not see me, and yet I found I could see what you were thinking – how frightened you were.

Suddenly I remembered what you said – that spirits can go through matter, I said, 'Here goes!' and ran at the door – and passed right through! It was the queerest thing I'd ever done. I tried it two or three times, just to see. When I got to the flat, Grandpa was in the room. I stayed by you all night. I got through to you the idea of head injury, but you thought 'concussion' – you would not recognise the truth.

Later on, a shining Eastern person [his mother's guide] appeared at the end of your bed. He wore a turban and a beard, and a sort of ray poured from his finger ends over your head, and you fell asleep. Your real self came out, so I told you what had happened, but you would not accept it when you woke.

Philip had been taught by his mother about the life beyond death. Because of this he was able to understand his situation and to see his grandfather, who had come to meet him. He remained close to his mother in the ensuing days, endeavouring to support her with his thoughts. It was a while before his confusion faded, but he was adjusting very quickly to the change and soon found happiness in the spirit dimension.

Lost and wandering

For others who die in similar circumstances the period of bewilderment and confusion may last a long time. If they have no concept of a spirit world or a life beyond, they have no means of grasping what has happened. Their distress may be such that the spirits who are trying to help cannot get through to them, rather in the way that it can be hard to get through to someone who is frozen in a state of shock. Such spirits are usually drawn back by their thoughts to their family or the place where they used to live, but sometimes they wander around the scene of the accident looking for someone to help them.

If someone who is psychic happens to come by, the spirit will be attracted to the light around them and follow it, just as a person lost in fog would follow someone with a lantern. The spirit remains attached to the psychic, while the psychic picks up the spirit's emotions. The psychic then wonders why they are feeling so disturbed.

Liz Leeke, a London medium, told me of an occasion when she and a trainee medium were walking together on their way to a Spiritualist church where they were to conduct a service. The trainee picked up feelings of depression and confusion. Fortunately, he realised that these feelings were emanating from an earthbound spirit. After the service, he and Liz sat down together and tuned in.

Liz told me, 'We became aware of a young man who had been knocked down on his bike and killed on the road where we had been walking. He said that he had been drawn to the medium because the medium reminded him of his brother. He was crying because he didn't know what had happened to him or where to go.

'We talked to him and explained the condition he was in. While we were doing this, a spirit woman came forward who said she was his aunt and he went off happily with her. We were so pleased to have been able to help him.'

In this instance, as in so many cases of rescue, the spirit was released very quickly and with very little effort on the part of the mediums. Once Liz and her colleague became aware of him, they were able to direct love and compassion towards him. This cleared his confusion. And then his aunt, who had probably been waiting, unseen, ever since the accident, was able to make herself known to him and to lead him away.

The live wire

Out-of-the-body experiences help us to understand what happens after death, as I discovered myself when staying in my uncle's house. Sylvan Muldoon, in his classic book *The Projection of the Astral Body*, describes a terrifying event in which he was almost killed.

One day after a storm he was walking with his brother and a friend along the street when they came across some electric power lines that had snapped. One of the wires was hanging from a pole across the street. Foolishly, Muldoon reached out to move the wire out of the way, not realising that it was live, and he was immediately knocked unconscious.

Next moment, he was aware of standing beside his physical body, looking down at it lying in the mud, still clinging to the wire. He felt the terrible pain of the electricity flowing through him but his astral or spirit body, just like his physical body, was rigid. He could see his companions, frightened dumb but afraid to touch him in case they, too, were electrocuted. He screamed out, 'Tell them to shut off the current!' But of course they were unable to hear him. Then, to his immense relief, he saw people rushing to his aid. A man reached down to help him up and, as he did so, Muldoon found himself inside his body once more.

The sequel to this event is significant. Muldoon writes:

> Almost every night, after this tragedy, I dreamed that I was being electrocuted, and in the dream I would live through the whole experience again, exactly as it happened ... On one occasion I awakened in this awful dream and found myself projected, living through the horrible experience exactly on the spot where it occurred, which was several blocks from my home.

Muldoon speculates about what might have happened had he died:

> Even had I become a resident of the unseen world, I should not be unlike I am now in the flesh; and by night, or whenever unconsciousness would overtake me, or when I would dream, I would live through my death, in the astral body, exactly as I lived through the experience in the astral body while still physically alive.

He concluded that he would then be earthbound, in a dim state of consciousness like that of someone having a nightmare. Every time he thought of the terror he would be drawn to the spot, re-enacting the events. And should anyone see him, they would claim that the site was haunted.

Murder!

There are many accounts of murder victims haunting the place where they were killed. This seems unjust. Why should the innocent victim be made to suffer? The sad truth is that an innocent person can become lost and confused for a time after dying, if the manner of their death was violent or traumatic.

There is, however, compassion in the spirit world for every spirit who is unhappy or in pain, and spirits who die through tragic circumstances are met with love. Even if their mental state is such that they cannot at first be reached, as soon as possible some loving spirit will take them into their care.

A favourite theme of ghost stories is the ghost who pursues their murderer from beyond the grave. There are instances of this happening in reality. In 1983 a young woman, Jacqueline Poole, was brutally murdered in her London flat. A few days later a medium called Christine Holohan began feeling a great sense of gloom. She knew that the spirit of a young woman had drawn close to her but it was a while before she realised that it was Jacqueline, whose death she had read about in the paper.

Christine told me, 'Jackie was distressed and very, very angry. She brought a great sense of urgency. She wasn't going anywhere until she had seen her murderer arrested. She followed me everywhere – she took over my life for a while. She kept urging me to go to the police. I told her I couldn't go to the police without evidence – they wouldn't believe me. So she gave me evidence.'

Jackie gave Christine the name of Hunt, her maiden

name, which had not been disclosed in any of the newspaper reports. She described the murder scene and gave her killer's nickname, which was 'Pokie'. Christine passed this information on to the police and it led to his arrest. The detective in charge of the case was impressed, admitting that there was no way in which Christine could have obtained these facts except from Jackie herself.

'Even then,' Christine said, 'Jackie didn't move on straight away. It was some time before she left me. But she did eventually go and I think she's at peace at last.'

This intense desire to see justice done is not felt by every murder victim. Some spirits, whatever the manner of their death, are readily able to forgive those responsible because, once they have passed over, they enter a state of spiritual understanding in which they can feel pity rather than hatred for the killer.

This was illustrated for me in a sitting I once did for the mother of a young man killed when he got involved in a fight at a pub. The fight was not her son's fault and the mother was determined to see the killer convicted, but he advised her to give up the struggle. 'Let it go,' he begged her. 'You don't have to do this for me.' His mother, however, refused to believe that he harboured no anger. She left still vowing to pursue the case to the bitter end.

I sympathised with her feelings. It was only natural that she should want to see the killer punished and, although I heard no more from her, I hope that she was eventually successful. But her son had found his peace and he did not wish to see his mother tormenting herself in a search for justice on his behalf.

I have already spoken of the importance of forgiveness, for those on both sides of life. Spirits who cannot forgive, even if they are the innocent victims of crime, may become earthbound by their hatred and anger. These emotions form a dark cloud around them that holds them back from entering the light. They have to learn to let go of the anger and leave the guilty party to God's justice. Only then can they progress. However, there is always help available to them from other spirits who constantly surround them with love, uplifting them and showing them how to find forgiveness within themselves.

The Rockland County Ghost

When someone dies in extreme fear and terror, these emotions can become so firmly imprinted on the mind that they cannot be shaken off. The victim continues to exist in a nightmare state, perhaps unaware that they are physically dead. An interesting example of this is given in *Ghost Hunter* by Hans Holzer.

In 1944 the newspaperman Danton Walker bought a dilapidated colonial-style mansion in Rockland County, New York. The house had been the scene of conflict, both in the American War of Independence and the Civil War. In 1779 it had been the headquarters of General Wayne at the time of the Battle of Stony Point. Walker spent a fortune renovating the house but when he moved in he found the psychic phenomena there – footsteps and banging on the front door – so alarming that he moved out again, into a small house in the grounds. He sensed that the mansion was haunted by the ghost of a Republican soldier and he called in the parapsychologist Hans Holzer to investigate.

Holzer visited the house, taking with him Eileen Garrett,

the leading medium of her day, and together with Walker and a psychiatrist identified in Holzer's account simply as 'Dr L', they held a séance. The medium went into a trance and her guide, Uvani, spoke through her, warning them that they were dealing with an entity who had been much hurt in life and who, at the time of his death, was not in his right mind.

Uvani allowed the spirit to take over the body of the medium. The spirit came through and was obviously full of pain and fear. He spoke in halting sentences, punctuated with weeping. The voice had a marked Polish accent. It was hard for the sitters to make sense of what he was saying, but slowly the tale emerged. The man was a Polish mercenary who had served with the Republican army. He had been captured and beaten to death by the English because he refused to reveal the whereabouts of some plans he had been carrying, which he had hidden nearby.

Holzer's graphic account of the séance reveals the man's tortured state of mind. Clearly terrified, he begged for protection, clinging to Dr L; he was attracted to the psychiatrist because he reminded him of his brother, who had also been killed. He had no sense of the time that had passed since his death. The battle seemed to him 'like yesterday'.

Uvani explained that the man was like someone passing in and out of a dream state, sometimes aware that he had died, sometimes thinking that he was still alive and in terrible pain. He removed the spirit from the medium, promising to take him 'to a kindlier dream'. The séance ended and peace returned to the house.

Death in war

The horrors of war extend beyond death. Victims of killing or torture, like the Polish soldier, may arrive on the other side of life so traumatised that they become trapped in their own terrifying recollections. Soldiers killed in the heat of battle die in a state of fear, surrounded by noise, confusion and the gruesome sights of the dead and dying. Their hearts may be filled with hatred towards the enemy. They carry these feelings over with them, while the collective emotions engendered by all those involved in the conflict create a dense fog around the scene of the battle. The spirits become lost in this fog, unable to find their way to the light.

Mediums have received many accounts from soldiers describing their experiences after death. Some of the most remarkable were published in *Lychgate* by Air Chief Marshal Hugh Dowding.

Lord Dowding, who was Commander-in-Chief of Fighter Command during the Battle of Britain, had an interest which would have caused his military colleagues to raise an eyebrow, had they known about it – he was a supporter of Spiritualism. During the Second World War he attended séances with leading mediums of the day, such as Estelle Roberts, during which deceased servicemen and women were reunited with the families they had left behind. Some of these spirits gave vivid accounts of what happened to them after leaving the body. In many cases, they did not realise that they had been killed and continued to fight alongside their living comrades. One said:

I didn't know that dying was like this. I thought it was all over and finished and sometimes we seemed to go through such a gruelling I didn't see as how we could stand any more, and then all of a sudden it ceased – and I was feeling as upright as a trivet ... I couldn't believe I was a 'gonner'. I saw my body just holed all over, and yet I couldn't believe it. I think I tried to pull it away from the gun, but there were others on top and beside me all in a heap. We'd got a direct hit all right.

The man saw his officer, who was as confused as he was, and asked him what they should do next.

'Load the gun, of course, you blighter,' ses he, just as he used to. I went to obey but, strong as I felt, I could not move the shells. They weren't so heavy as all that but I could not get hold of them, they were slippery. I tell the officer and he comes along to help, cursing proper he was by this time ...

Lots of 'shadowy' people joined them. He saw the battle going on but the enemy couldn't see him. He found that he was floating as if his feet wouldn't stay on the ground. Still not aware that he was dead, he knelt down and prayed. As he did so he saw a man who looked like an Arab and wondered how a civilian had got on to the battlefield. The Arab was one of the rescuers who go into such situations to meet those passing over and, whenever possible, help them into the light. The Arab told the soldier that he had come to take him to Christ.

I looked to where the others were but I could see nothing but a blinding glorious light, it seemed to fill my head and burn through something that was keeping me there and then the voice spoke again, something like this: 'By your sacrifice you have attained to the Crown of Fortitude' – and then I remember no more. That was the last I saw on earth.

The RAF pilot

It should not be assumed that every soldier dying in such terrible conditions suffers similar confusion. Sometimes, even in the midst of conflict, the passing can be gentle.

Lesley Garton, a Dorset medium, has given me this account, relayed to her by a First World War pilot called George:

> I was in the plane one second and the next I was outside floating. At first I thought that I must have bailed out. The plane was crashed below me. Then I saw that nothing was happening. I was not going down. My body had disappeared. I was puzzled and thought I was dreaming. The time went by and the sky became a wonderful shade of blue and I was aware that there was some kind of activity going on around me. A voice said, 'Come along old son, it's no good hanging around here, time to move.' Then I felt whisked through some kind of vacuum and found myself among people I knew had died. This was my first recognition of death.

Wherever there is war and bloodshed, spirits are flung into the spirit world unprepared. Many find their way safely home but others become lost. Those who bring about war carry the responsibility not only for the suffering they cause to the living but also for that they cause to the departed.

This is a sobering thought – one that should make us all pray earnestly for peace to come to our troubled world, and for all hatred and violence to cease.

11
Evil Spirits

Evil spirits are, in my view, those who have deliberately and knowingly turned their backs on the light. Their whole purpose is to bring hatred and destruction into the world and to smother the light in others.

When I first started doing spirit release I was unaware that such spirits existed. One medium assured me glibly, 'There's no such thing as an evil spirit.'

It would be nice if that were true, but unfortunately it is not. I have stressed how unusual it is to encounter anything evil. In fact, in all the years I have been performing this work I have only come across three or four cases where I would say that the forces involved were evil. In those cases, however, I was in no doubt that I was in danger. The power and malice I felt directed towards me was so strong that I needed all my strength, and the protection of my guides, to shield me from it. Any medium who undertakes spirit release needs to be aware of the existence of evil or they may find themselves under attack when they least expect it.

The spirit who wouldn't go away

Some years ago I had a phone call from a woman called Margaret. She told me that there was a poltergeist in her house and asked if she could come and see me to get my advice. From what she told me it didn't sound like a very serious case, so I willingly agreed. Little did I know what I was letting myself in for.

A couple of hours before Margaret was due to arrive, I started feeling agitated, bad-tempered and irritable. I wondered why I was feeling like that; then I became aware of a male spirit hovering around me. Sensing that he belonged to Margaret and that he was earthbound, I sat down in my sanctuary and tried to talk to him.

In my usual way, I sent him compassion, telling him to go to the light. All I received in reply was a distinct feeling of hostility, accompanied by language of the sort you wouldn't expect to hear from a spiritual being. I persevered for some time but I was getting nowhere. So I left him to the guides and went off to do something else.

When Margaret arrived, he was still there. I told her what had happened, toning down the language a little. She recognised him as her father, who had been abusive and a drunkard. Not surprisingly, she didn't want to hear from him. But he had a forceful personality and kept intruding into my thoughts, making it difficult for Margaret's mother, whom she had loved, to get through.

The sitting was not a success and I knew that Margaret was disappointed. She left – but her father didn't. For the rest of the day I felt him following me around. I sat down in my sanctuary again and tried to persuade him to leave, but he wouldn't go. His energy was building up powerfully in the room. By this time I was becoming anxious. I had another sitter coming that evening and I knew that, with his malign presence around me, I would not be able to communicate clearly with that sitter's loved ones. Summoning up all my energy, and calling upon the guides and the holy angels of light, I commanded him to leave.

At that point the guides stepped forward. This was a case when they, so to speak, took a spirit by the scruff of the neck. They sent him off to wherever they decided he should go and peace descended upon my room once more. It was a salutary lesson to me never to take anything for granted in this work, but to be alert for the dangers that can sometimes lurk under the surface in the most seemingly simple cases.

Deceptive spirits

Evil spirits can be cunning and deceptive. They don't always reveal their presence by making a noise or throwing things around. Their methods are more subtle and therefore more dangerous. They play upon the minds of their victims. Sometimes they disguise themselves as benign spirits or as lost souls in need of help. In this way they win their victims' sympathy and can gain a hold upon them that is hard to break. One of the worst examples I have come across was the case of a girl called Vanessa.

Vanessa was about twenty. She was intelligent and highly sensitive but she was also quite lonely and found it hard to make friends. She was keen on developing her natural psychic ability and meditated regularly. One day, while meditating, she became aware of the spirit of a young man who spoke to her in her mind, telling her that he had been murdered. She felt sorry for him and wanted to help, so she opened her mind to him, encouraging him to come closer. She told no one about this man but, every day when she meditated, she communicated with him. He gave her information about his life, indicating that he had been unhappy and misunderstood. He said that he loved her and a strong bond developed between them.

But the spirit was not what he seemed. Gradually, his personality began to change. He became more demanding of her time and attention. It was as though he was trying to control her life, encouraging her to spend more and more time alone so that she could be with him. Friends noticed the change in her, asking why she was becoming strange and withdrawn, but there was no one she could confide in. Realising at last that she was in the grip of something evil, she tried to pull away – but by this time he had established such a hold over her that she couldn't get him out of her thoughts.

It was at this point that she went to a medium for help. In fact, she went to several mediums. All of them succeeded in freeing her from her tormentor for a short time; then he would come back again. The problem was that, at some level, she didn't really want him to go. She was aware that she was dabbling in something dangerous but she was fascinated by him – and enjoying all the attention she was getting. As soon as one of the mediums sent him away she would draw him back again by her thoughts.

When she came to see me, I advised her that she had to take responsibility for herself. She needed to tell him to go – and to mean it. I also suggested that she find other things to fill her life, so that she didn't have so much time to dwell on him. The advice was not welcome but, happily, shortly afterwards she found a boyfriend, which gave her the strength to end the attachment.

Possession

There are many horror stories involving possession – stories that are usually wildly exaggerated and sensationalised. Possession is a state in which a spirit entity completely takes over a person's mind and body. This is an extremely rare occurrence. It is hard enough for spirits of any sort just to get through to a living person, let alone take them over! There are, however, some well-authenticated cases of possession. One of the most famous is known as the Watseka Wonder.

In 1865 a girl called Mary Roff died in Watseka, Illinois, in a fit of insanity. Thirteen years later another Watseka girl, Lurancy Vennum, a stranger to the Roff family, also became insane. The doctor treating her identified a number of spirits who were apparently possessing the girl, the chief of which was Mary Roff. Mary's mother, who was present while the doctor was examining Lurancy, asserted that she recognised her daughter and unwisely advised Lurancy to allow Mary to control her, which she agreed to do.

For the next four months, Mary was in constant possession of Lurancy's body. She asked to be taken 'home' – to the house of Mary's parents. There, she behaved exactly like their dead daughter, recognising every object in the house and every one of Mary's friends. She was able to describe incidents in Mary's life of which Lurancy could have had no knowledge. At the end of the four months

Mary announced that she was to leave Lurancy's body. She bade a tearful goodbye to her family and fell into a trance. When she awoke, Lurancy was back. Thereafter, Mary took over for short periods from time to time, but never again did she exert such total control.

Invasion of the mind

The Watseka Wonder is an example of the most unusual and extreme type of possession. But there are other cases in which a spirit can invade a person's mind, affecting their moods and leading them to behave in ways that are out of character. This could be called partial or temporary possession. It can happen when the spirit has a very strong, dominant personality and the person to whom they are seeking to attach themselves is vulnerable or weak-willed. It can also happen when, as in Vanessa's case, the person deliberately opens their mind to the spirit, perhaps because they want to help them.

Immense harm can be done even by a spirit who has no evil intent, but is just clinging, in their loneliness, to someone who seems to them to hold out some hope of assistance or companionship.

Hazel Denning, in *True Hauntings*, tells the story of a young man called Chris whose close friend, Perry, took his own life. From that time on Chris began to feel deeply depressed and suicidal. He was aware that these feelings were coming from Perry but felt that Perry was trying to get through to him and that he had to help him.

A couple of weeks later, Chris was involved in a car accident in which he suffered a broken collar bone. But the accident might have been much worse. He claimed that, as he had been driving, something grabbed the steering wheel and crashed the car into a telephone pole. He was convinced that Perry was trying to kill him.

He consulted Hazel Denning. She explained that, in all probability, Perry had no malice towards Chris, but wanted him to join him in the world beyond death. Chris realised that he couldn't allow his friend to influence him in this way. He spoke to Perry, telling him to go into the light. He was sad to part from his friend, but as soon as he had done so, his depression lifted.

Vulnerability to spirit invasion

Perry was not an evil spirit, only misguided. But evil spirits deliberately exert their will over anyone they can influence, in order to try to make them carry out their wishes. From time to time one hears of murderers or people who commit violent crimes and claim that they were compelled to act by forces beyond their control, or that they heard voices in their heads telling them what to do.

Some of these criminals may indeed be the victims of evil spirits. However, that does not exonerate them. Evil spirits can only manipulate those who have darkness within themselves. They are drawn to individuals who harbour hatred or malice and play upon these emotions.

Drugs and alcohol make a person more receptive psychically and therefore more prone to invasion. The more someone becomes dependent on these substances (and an evil spirit will encourage the dependency), the less resistance they have to the spirit's influence.

Ouija boards are also extremely dangerous. These boards, which are sometimes regarded as a game, or as an easy and amusing way of establishing contact with the spirit world, are an open invitation to any spirit who happens to be hovering around to have a go at getting through. If the spirit is a benevolent one, no harm is done, although it is a cumbersome means of communication and produces a meaningless jumble of letters more often than a coherent message.

Evil spirits, however, view ouija board sessions as a chance to have some fun. The people using the board may have no psychic awareness and therefore cannot sense that the energy around them is of a negative kind. They do not realise that, in attempting to communicate in this way, they are creating a channel for the spirits to use – a channel that they may find very hard to close again.

Those whose minds are damaged by mental illness or imbalance can also be vulnerable to the intrusion of spirits who are not necessarily evil, but who perhaps are lost and confused. A patient who complains of hearing voices may be under the influence of earthbound spirits, although these voices are often combined and confused with voices from their own subconscious.

Today, there are just a few psychiatrists who recognise this situation. This is an encouraging trend, especially when such psychiatrists are willing to consult mediums to assist in the treatment of the patient. The medium can contact and remove the spirit, something that the psychiatrist, unless he has psychic ability, may be unable to do. The psychiatrist can then cure the patient, healing the wounds in the psyche and strengthening the mind so that the patient is able to resist further attacks.

However, in case all this sounds alarming, let me add a word of reassurance. We all have a natural defence mechanism that safeguards us from invasion by spirits, evil or otherwise. No one can be taken over or possessed unless, at some level, they invite this or allow it to happen.

Spirit 'hooligans'

Evil spirits are attracted to areas where there is any kind of negativity. Take, for instance, a housing estate in a depressed area where there is a high level of crime, drug taking, unemployment and all the ills that go with it. If you could see such a place from the spirit world you would see any number of earthbound spirits in that location. These are people who used to live there. After death, they remain in the same place because they have nothing better to do. I am not, of course, implying for one moment that everyone who lives on a troubled housing estate becomes earthbound when they die. What I am saying is that these conditions create an environment in the spiritual dimension that mirrors the environment here.

Most of these earthbound spirits are lost and confused rather than evil. However, evil spirits do take advantage of them and try to control them. They are like gangsters or hooligans who recruit weak-willed or idle individuals and incite them to commit crimes in which they would not otherwise have been involved.

A house in such an area where members of the family are psychic draws such spirits like a magnet, because they know that there is energy available that they can use. If they find they can have an amusing time by frightening the residents, they will invite all their friends in – and then you have a real problem on your hands! Add other factors, such as disturbed teenagers, and tension and antagonism within the family, and you have a recipe for disaster.

A house full of spirits

Some mediums, more courageous than I am, specialise in dealing with such cases. Leslie Moul from Bournemouth is an expert in dealing with extreme cases of attack by dark forces. One evening he had an emergency call to go to the house of a local family who were being plagued by violent poltergeist activity. The call was made by the family's social worker, who had some knowledge of mediumship and realised that the services of a strong medium were urgently required.

When Leslie arrived he found the police already on the scene. One of the policemen, however, was making a rapid exit. He told Leslie, 'You're braver than I am, going in there. It's a madhouse!'

It was indeed a scene of pandemonium. Leslie told me, 'Crockery was flying around. The furniture was moving. Two terrified policemen were pinned to the wall by a heavy Welsh dresser. A pipe leading from the gas meter had been pulled off the wall and tied in a knot! It was the worst case I had ever seen.

'We got the policemen free and gradually the energy started to calm down. I could see the spirits. The main one was a drug addict who had lived in the vicinity. He didn't realise he was dead and thought he was still on a trip. He couldn't understand why no one could see him. Other earthbound spirits had been drawn in by the energy and they were adding to it.'

The spirits were removed and Leslie discovered that the tremendous level of energy that had built up in the house had been caused by a variety of circumstances. There were two teenage children, both slightly disturbed. The mother was an alcoholic and the father a drug addict. But the problem had been sparked off by the mother dabbling with a ouija board. Leslie advised the family to move out of the house for a month. They did so, and when they returned, there were no more phenomena.

Jessica

Some earthbound spirits fall victim to evil spirits who prevent them from finding their way to the light. One sad and moving case I came across concerned a young drug addict called Jessica who took her own life.

I was asked to go to the house of my friend Ann, whom I have mentioned before. Ann told me that the spirit of a teenage girl had taken up residence in her house. She was picking up feelings of great fear and anxiety. A visitor who was psychic had even seen the girls's face superimposed upon Ann's. Ann was particularly aware of the spirit in her bedroom at night, which was making it hard for her to sleep. She couldn't think who the teenager could be but she felt she needed help to deal with her. So she called me in.

When I gave the spirit's name as Jessica, Ann was able to identify her as a friend of her son's, a girl of about 18 who had been on drugs and had taken her own life. Ann's son did not take drugs himself but he had befriended Jessica and tried to help her. Because of this, Jessica, in her earth-bound state, had initially been drawn to him, before attaching herself to Ann because she saw a light around her.

Jessica was weeping when she came through to me. She had endured a desperately unhappy life. Her parents had disowned her and she had lived on the streets, turning to crime to get money to satisfy her addiction. When she died she had been caught up with a group of evil spirits who had been present in the place from which she used to obtain her drugs. These spirits were terrorising her. They told her that she was wicked and that, if she went away from them, she would be sent to hell. Because she was not really a bad person, she was full of guilt and remorse, so she believed them. But she felt safe with Ann, particularly when she was in Ann's bedroom, where there was a loving energy that gave her protection.

The guides came through strongly, telling Jessica that there was nothing for her to fear and that she was not going to be punished. They surrounded her with love, driving away the evil spirits who had tormented her. There was a great sense of joy and relief as she was taken away. The light was waiting for her, and in that light were loved ones from her own family, who were going to take care of her.

Exorcism

The Christian church has always sought to remove spirits using the rite of exorcism. Following the example of Jesus, who drove out what the Bible calls 'unclean spirits', they endeavour to drive the spirit away with the ritual of 'bell, book and candle'. Ringing the bell echoes the ringing of bells for departed spirits, shutting the book (the Bible) excludes the soul from the word of God and dousing the candle snuffs out the light of the doomed soul.

Mediums regard this approach as cruel – as well as showing ignorance of the spiritual world. It assumes that all spirits around those on earth are evil, making no distinction between evil spirits and those which are earthbound and in need of release.

Some clergymen today prefer to talk of deliverance rather than exorcism. This is a gentler approach, but it is nevertheless concerned with delivering the victim from attack by a spirit entity rather than recognising the needs of the spirit itself. In fact, most clergymen are reluctant to get involved in the field at all and prefer to attribute cases of haunting, possession or intrusion to psychological problems.

Calling in a priest or vicar to sort out a haunted house can sometimes make the situation worse. The church represents moral authority. The spirit, who may not in any case have been a Christian, is not likely to take kindly to a priest trying to expel it and may react by causing even more disturbance. Clergymen undertaking this task who have no psychic ability run the risk of having the spirit attach itself to them and follow them home.

Mediums seldom speak of performing exorcisms. Their objective is not to drive the spirit away but to release it – preferably into the light, but, if this is not possible, then into the charge of the guides who will deal with it as they think best. Exorcism is only used in cases where the spirit is not amenable to being helped and has to be removed.

Exorcism is extremely difficult, demanding and dangerous work, but some mediums have a special calling for it. One of the best known of these is Philip Steff, who lives in Bath. Philip has carried out rescue work for over thirty years. He has appeared many times on television and been featured in a number of books. He sees exorcism as a distinct aspect of his work. It needs a different approach, as he explained to me.

'Exorcisms tend to be more violent. You have to meet the issue head on. Psychic attack is very real and should never be underestimated. Entities are clever, deceptive and capable of causing considerable harm. They have to be sent back to wherever they came from.'

Philip's chief guide, Otto, was a Prussian officer when on earth. A strong character who stands no nonsense, his firmness and strength is often needed in dealing with entities who are obstinate and determined to resist. One of Philip's most memorable cases concerned a family consisting of a mother, Katherine, her daughter and her two sons. The brothers had spent some time in America where they became involved with a satanic cult. When they tried to pull away, the cult members threatened that they would be physically attacked.

When the brothers returned to England it became clear that this was no empty threat. By this time, both of them were ill. One, who was six feet tall, had lost weight until he was just seven stone. The other had suffered a stroke leading to brain damage. Both of them had found lacerations like whip marks which had appeared on their backs. In despair, Katherine called in Philip.

On the day before Philip's visit, she telephoned the friends with whom he was staying to check what time he planned to arrive. A few minutes before her call, the door of the living room in Philip's friends' house burst open and an icy blast filled the room. Philip took it as a sign of things to come and decided to take a couple of other mediums with him for support.

The mediums arrived at the house and were given a meal. Even while they were eating they were aware that they were under psychic attack and a couple of them experienced a smell like human excrement. After dinner, while Philip was talking with the family, Katherine gave a look of horror and exclaimed, 'There's something in here – something black!'

Philip became aware of a shape like a large black bird bearing down upon him. Challenging the entity to do its worst, he backed towards it, symbolically trapping it against the window. When he looked round he 'saw' clair-voyantly an outline of the bird's shape, as if it had gone through the window.

The mediums took a much-needed break, refreshing themselves with a swim in the local swimming pool. It was going to be a long night. That evening, they prepared for the exorcism. Philip used the dining-room table as an altar, setting up a cross, candles and a Bible. Each member of the family was given a crucifix which had been blessed with holy water to wear. He called upon the archangels of light and, with the aid of the guides, the mediums gave healing to all the family.

Like many exorcists, Philip uses candles, holy water and other tools for their symbolic value, though he warns that they have no power in themselves. The real power to banish the spirit must come from the guides, from the spiritual strength and faith of the mediums and, ultimately, from God himself. This exorcism, like most of those he has carried out (he frankly admits that not every case is successful), brought about a complete change in the family.

The brothers' health was restored and the house was cleared.

No lasting condemnation

Such spirits represent the dangerous side of spirit release work and serve as a warning that the world beyond death, just like ours, contains both good and evil, darkness and light. Yet even these spirits have some spark of divinity deep inside them, and the possibility always remains open that they can renounce evil and turn towards God again. Their ascent back into the light may take aeons of time, but they are never condemned – unless they choose to condemn themselves.

I want now to turn to a slightly different aspect of spirit release: rescue circles, and how they are used by the guides as a means of helping spirits in need.

12

Rescue Circles

I have spoken about visiting houses or sites in order to release spirits who are trapped there. Sometimes, however, the guides bring earthbound spirits to a medium. This can happen when a medium is sitting quietly in their own home or while they are giving a consultation to a client. And there are also groups known as rescue circles, where mediums meet together on a regular basis in order to do spirit release work. This is very rewarding – but it is definitely not for the amateur or the faint-hearted.

The possessive mother

Many years ago, when I first started giving private sittings at home, I would sometimes notice that, among the spirits who came to communicate, there were one or two who seemed different from the others. They reminded me of the ghosts I had seen in my childhood home. Sometimes I saw them like dark shadows. They hovered around the sitter or stood in a corner of the room. There was no light or joy about them. I soon learned that these were earthbound spirits.

Some of these spirits were attached to the sitters because of a deep emotional bond that existed between them. I gave an example of this earlier, when talking about Joan and her father, explaining how his remorse had kept him earthbound until he was able, through making contact with her, to ask her forgiveness.

Sitters are usually unaware of such spirits but they invariably complain of feeling depressed, angry or uneasy, or of experiencing some other emotion that they cannot account for. They are, of course, being affected subconsciously by whatever the spirit is feeling. Once the contact is made and the spirit released, they return to their normal state of mind. Some sitters, however, do realise the nature of their problem and have come to me so that I can help them with it.

Robert was a successful businessman. His father had died young and, being a dutiful son, he had taken on the task of looking after his mother, Shirley. This became an increasing burden over the years, even more so as she became partially disabled but refused to accept help from anyone but him. Although he made allowances because of her health, he resented the fact that she was unnaturally clinging and tried to interfere in and dominate every aspect of his life.

He came to see me a few months after his mother died. Guiltily, he admitted that he had been relieved when she passed away, hoping that he could now get on with his life in peace. But since her death, nothing had gone right for him. He had lost his self-confidence and his career was suffering as a consequence. He had become withdrawn and often didn't even want to go out of the house. He wondered whether his mother had become a malign influence, punishing him for not loving her enough.

I tuned in to his mother, whom I sensed standing behind him. I was unprepared for the rush of emotion that swept over me. I had never felt a spirit so anxious and fearful. It became clear to me what had happened. Shirley had loved her son, but it had been a possessive love that smothered him and was smothering him still. Since she had died she had clung to him. Just as in life, she was afraid that if she let him slip out of her grasp, she would lose him. Robert's long-dead father was there beside her but either she couldn't see him or she was ignoring him. All her attention was focused on Robert. She was, unknowingly, affecting him with her fear and draining his energy.

Fortunately, the guides were able to persuade her to let go of that paralysing emotion. She turned to her husband, who convinced her to go with him. Before she left, I had to promise her that she could return to visit Robert whenever she wished. Robert wasn't too happy with the idea. But I explained that once she had made the transition to the spirit world, she would come back with a different attitude because she would be happy and would have other things in her new spiritual home to occupy her.

The nanny

Some of the earthbound spirits brought to me by the guides are attached not to the sitters personally but to the houses where they live. When I sense that this is the case, I ask the sitter if they have felt a presence in their home or experienced any kind of psychic activity there. Almost invariably, the answer is 'yes'.

I used to wonder how it was possible for the guides to

bring earthbound spirits from the houses they were haunting to my house. It was explained to me that since they are in a semi-conscious state, they can be carried along like sleepwalkers. I often sense the bewilderment such spirits are feeling, wondering where they are and how they got there. But the fact that they have been brought out of their familiar environment and into my home is an important stage in their release. The light that exists in my room helps to bring them to a state of full consciousness and makes them aware that they have been earthbound, and the guides can then lead them away.

Nicola worked at an old people's home, where she had a flat at the top of the building. She had been aware of the spirit of an old woman. Several other members of staff had also felt the presence and been frightened by it. Nicola was not frightened. She sensed that the old woman had taken a liking to her, and even felt her tuck her up in bed at night! But she was concerned that the spirit wasn't happy and needed to be released. When Nicola came to me for a sitting she asked whether I could visit the home. As it was a long way from where I live, I suggested that we ask the guides if the spirit could be brought to us instead.

My first impression, as I became aware of the old woman, was that she used to be a patient in the home. But I quickly realised I was mistaken and asked whether she could have worked there. Nicola told me that before the building had been converted into a residential home, it had been a family house. Partly through my psychic impressions and partly through Nicola's knowledge of the history of the building, we were able to piece together the story.

The woman had been a nanny, looking after the children of the family. She had no one of her own. She had been very religious and couldn't understand why, when she died, she hadn't found herself in heaven. This confusion had prevented her from moving on. As she had such a strong sense of duty she had remained in the house, trying in her own way to continue her responsibility of caring by looking after the residents, as well as Nicola. She was desperate for someone to notice her and she attached herself to Nicola, sensing that she was aware of her presence. Because of this attachment, the guides had been able to bring her along when Nicola came for her sitting.

After Nicola and I had sat for a few minutes, talking to the woman and projecting love towards her, I had the impression of her symbolically packing her bags to leave the home.

'What a waste of all those years,' she said to me in my mind. 'Staying here and I didn't need to. Wandering up and down the stairs and in and out of the rooms and nobody able to see me. I tried to help but, of course, I couldn't do anything. They don't need me there now.'

My eyes filled with tears as I experienced her emotion. 'Can you see a light?' I asked her. She replied that she could and I felt her move towards it.

Nicola whispered softly, 'God bless her on her journey.' She felt that a weight had been lifted from her. A few days later, she phoned me to say that the home and her flat now felt light and clear.

Working alone

I have a room in my house set aside where I do sittings, and this room I call my sanctuary. Over the years, an energy has built up in this room which facilitates communication. I see it as a place where the veil between the worlds is thinner.

Sometimes while I am sitting there alone, a spirit is brought to me who is in need of help. When this happens, it is not important for me to know anything about the spirit or where it came from. All I do is focus my mind upon it and send it love and compassion. Sometimes I speak to these spirits, sometimes there is no need for words. After a few minutes the feeling of sadness and heaviness they bring with them lifts. There is a familiar surge of energy and joy and I know that they have found their way home.

A number of mediums work in this quiet way. One of them is Lesley Garton. Her guide is George, the First World War pilot whom she released (see Chapter 10). Lesley started doing rescue work in 1982, while she was sitting in a development circle. She would communicate with the spirits in a state of light trance and relay what they were saying to the leader of the group, who would encourage them to go towards the light. George was one of these spirits. After his release he chose to remain with her so that they could work together.

Some time later Lesley had to leave the circle for family reasons, but she continued to meditate regularly, progressing on her inner spiritual journey. One day George asked her if she would take up her rescue work again, with his help. Lesley wrote to me:

I have been brought many discarnate souls who were victims of sudden death and have been stuck between the dimensions. I must strongly emphasise the rarity of this. I feel a shadow of their distress and pain and sometimes it takes a little time but all make a successful transition. The guides bring the soul forward and apparently they see my substance as lighter and then merge into it to relive their final moments, to trigger the immediate release into the greater light of the higher dimension.

Lesley comments, 'They need a body to do this.' This is something I have found to be true in my own experience. These spirits who have been flung out of their physical form so abruptly need the sensation of being in touch with a body once more. The process they go through is akin to that of a psychiatric patient who is regressed to a time when they experienced a trauma, and encouraged to relive that trauma in their mind in order that they can release it. Rescue work can be seen as a kind of therapy for spirits!

Reliving the spirit's trauma

Taking on the condition of the spirits in this way generally involves no more than picking up a mild impression of the sensations they experienced at the end of their lives. For instance, a person who died of a heart attack might give the medium a brief sensation of pain in the heart. But sometimes the medium is required to take on more fully the spirit's memory of its passing, and this can be both painful and harrowing.

The following account appeared in *Light*, the journal of the College of Psychic Studies (Summer 1987). It was contributed by the late Eddie Burks, a medium with a long experience of helping spirits in this way, and it describes his sensations as he carries out a rescue:

I am getting a pain in the back of my head. This is someone who died preceded by a very intense pain at the back of the skull. Very unpleasant. Oh, it is intense! I seldom get such a degree of discomfort as this. I can put my finger on the very spot where it is radiating. Oh, it is quite exhausting. I think it is a broken neck. The neck is broken and I think the person concerned couldn't move and of course suffered this very violent pain ... passed on in a state of agony and has not let go of it ...

There is a feeling of panic with this as well as pain and complete impotence. I seem to be lying face down with my head on one side bent towards the right ... my head in an unnatural position underneath the body, the tendons pulling the head down.

Eddie became aware that the spirit was a teenage girl who had been killed in a potholing accident, two or three years previously.

All this time she has suffered this pain. She died with it so impressed upon her that nothing else can come through. How awful. The panic and the horror. The impotence and the panic were a dreadful combination. This is why I have been carrying this pain. I have got to drain it off her and Andrew [Eddie's guide] knows I don't mind putting up with it so he has brought her along ...

Now we come to the part where we have to project love and light towards her ... my head is being filled with it ... and it isn't just her, it is those who have been trying to help her. There is a feeling almost of exaltation that this has worked. There are a number of people around her now all working very hard. They are so full of joy because they can see she is being released. Oh, what joy! She has enlisted a great deal of compassion amongst those who are now helping her ... We send her our love. The pain is fading.

Places of power

Wherever prayer, meditation and healing are performed – in places such as a church, a psychic centre, a healing clinic or a private sanctuary – a light and energy is built up. The rescuers take advantage of this to help earthbound spirits. Those on earth who visit or use such places generally have no idea that this work is going on in the invisible dimension, nor is it necessary for them to know.

Many spirits can be helped without the intervention of a medium. The guides simply bring them to a place of power, much as we on earth might bring a person who was sick or troubled to a church or sanctuary in order to give them spiritual healing. I sometimes wonder what goes on in my own sanctuary after I have left and closed the door! I am happy to think that the work I have done there has helped create an environment in which troubled spirits can find peace.

Spiritualist churches are also used by the rescuers in this way. Like churches of all religions, Spiritualists often complain of dwindling numbers in the congregation; although, having said that, many churches are well attended and flourishing. However, if the people attending the church were able to see plainly into the invisible world, they would see the church full of spirit beings. Most of them are relatives and loved ones of members of the congregation and there are others who, just like people on earth, come out of curiosity to see what is going on.

Earthbound spirits may wander in as well, drawn by the light and sensing that perhaps there may be an opportunity for them to make contact with someone who can understand their plight. The medium, intent on taking the service and communicating with the loved ones, does not often observe these poor spirits and the congregation is quite unaware of them. Yet the guides are doing their work and this too is an environment in which many such spirits can be released.

My home circle

For many years I have run a spiritual circle. This is not a rescue circle as such. It is simply a group in which I sit, with about half a dozen close friends who are mediums and healers, for meditation and discussion – as well as a cup of tea and a chat afterwards! However, from time to time, earthbound spirits are brought to the group. Sometimes these are in some way connected with a patient or client of one of the circle members, but on other occasions there is no link that we are aware of.

The great advantage for a medium, carrying out rescue work within such a situation, is that they have the support of the other group members. A stronger energy is generated which enables the spirit to be released more quickly and easily. When working within the group, I use the technique described by Lesley, that of going into a light trance and speaking on behalf of the spirit. At this point I am experiencing the spirit's emotions, and probably crying with it, though in no sense am I possessed by it. I am fully aware of what is taking place and could, if I wished, break off the contact at any time.

As I express the spirit's words and feelings, another member of the group will talk to it, endeavouring to find out what is troubling it. They will urge the spirit to look for a light and to go towards it, putting itself into the hands of the guides who are there to help. These rescues are often very moving and, by the time they are finished, I am not the only one with tears in my eyes!

Rescue in Exeter

There are many rescue circles all over the country, and indeed the world. They work with great dedication, seeking neither payment nor publicity. Their work consists both of travelling to houses or other places where hauntings are reported and also of sitting regularly together, usually in the home of one of the members, in order to make themselves available to help any spirits the circle guides bring to them.

The spirits may be those of people who died in the area where the circle is held but, as distance is immaterial to the spirit dimension, they can be brought from anywhere, even another part of the world. When there is a natural disaster, such as a flood or an earthquake, many spirits who have been thrown into the spirit world in a state of panic or distress are brought to such groups for rescue. Victims of man-made catastrophes, such as wars or terrorist attacks, may also be brought along.

Michael Evans, who lives in Exeter, runs a rescue circle which meets in his home. Although he himself is not a medium, he acts as a recorder and speaks to the spirits as they come through the mediums.

The group started its work in 1991 when the guides asked them if they would be willing to undertake the rescue of soldiers killed in the Gulf War, which had just begun. They agreed, and a young US Air Force pilot came through, explaining that he and his crew knew that they had died – they had seen their bodies in the plane. In spite of having been killed they were quite cheerful and asked the hostess, 'Could we sit on your settee, ma'am? Gee, we like your lounge.'

The group had no problem explaining to them that although they had left their physical bodies, they could look forward to an interesting life in a new dimension and that they must mentally ask for help and look for the light that would appear.

With the war raging, the group was kept busy dealing with those killed on both sides of the conflict. These included a number of Iraqis who could speak English. The circle was their first contact after the shock and injury of their death and many were puzzled and confused.

One voice with an Iraqi accent asked plaintively: 'Where is the paradise? I cannot find paradise. Where are the maidens? Where are all the beautiful things?' He felt let down because he had not found himself in the Afterlife promised by his religion.

When the Gulf War ended, the group, who by this time had gained considerable experience in helping lost spirits, were asked if they would continue to do rescue work. They willingly agreed. Over the years they have helped a great variety of spirits who have been earthbound for many different reasons. One was a member of the court of Queen Victoria who had slept for most of the time since his death, since he had died convinced that he would sleep in the tomb until the

Last Trump. Another was a young girl who reported that she was cold and in a dark box underground. She was imprisoned by the idea of a coffin and sleeping in the grave. When, by persuasion, she was shown how to break free from her self-imposed prison, her happiness was mirrored on the face of the medium through whom she was speaking.

Jack, the non-believer

Michael found that an effective method of helping earthbound spirits was to ask them if there was a particular person they loved who they would like to come and meet them. He discovered that if this was suggested to such spirits, and if they were asked to concentrate on a person they had loved, the guides would often bring that person forward. A spirit ignorant of the spiritual dimension might be more comfortable with the idea of going with someone they recognised than with that of going into a light. Michael has employed this method very successfully in numerous cases. A typical example was Jack, who had died, like so many others, with no concept that there was anything beyond.

Speaking through one of the mediums, he said in a puzzled voice, 'I'm not where I ought to be. I ought to be at home with my missus but for some reason I'm not there any more.'

'What happened to you?' Michael asked him.

'I don't know. First I was there then I wasn't.' Belligerently, he went on, 'I don't believe all that rubbish you've been spouting here. When you die you're just put in a box, aren't you?'

'If you're in a box,' Michael pointed out, 'how can you be talking to us? Your physical body has been put in a box but your spirit's here.'

'Then why aren't I there with it?' Jack complained. 'I don't understand. I just want to go home!'

Michael asked him if there was anyone he would like to talk to. After some thought, Jack said that he would like to talk to his mother. 'But if they're dead,' he asked, 'how can I talk to them?'

'Would you like to see your mother again?' Michael asked.

'I don't see how I can,' Jack replied, adding, 'I know but I don't know' – a remark that indicated that he did, at some level, understand that he had died.

Still, he was unconvinced. 'A relative used to go to a medium,' he told Michael. 'I didn't believe a word of it. I thought she was dotty. Oh gawd, she was right!'

Soon, both Jack's mother and father came to collect him and he went off with them, a changed man.

A note of caution

I said at the beginning of this chapter that rescue circles are not for the amateur or the faint-hearted. It can be distressing to listen to a spirit, speaking through a medium, describing in vivid detail the manner of their death. And it can be even more distressing if, as the medium, you are helping them relive their agonies.

There is also a danger that, if the members of the circle are not sufficiently cautious or experienced, an earthbound spirit may be brought to the circle whom they find themselves unable to release. Having been brought to the group, the spirit will not go back where it came from. It will attach itself to a member of the group, or take up residence in their home or in the house where the group is held. For this reason, I would not advise anyone to sit in a rescue circle without proper training.

In fact, as you will by now have gathered, it is necessary to adopt a cautious approach when dealing with earth-bound spirits of any kind. The more psychic or sensitive a person is, the more they should be aware of the need for protection. And it is the subject of psychic protection that I am now going to address.

13

Psychic Protection

I would like to begin by stressing what I said in a previous chapter. We all have a natural defence system that protects us from any spirit that might attempt to invade the mind or harm us in any way. This is the aura or energy field that surrounds us. The more a person is grounded in the physical world, the stronger is their defence. In fact, someone whose mind is focused on material things probably has no perception of the spiritual world and no spirit being will be able to penetrate their consciousness.

However, sensitive people, especially if they are psychics or mediums, have auras that provide less protection. Although they are receptive to loving spirits such as guides, relatives and friends who are around them, which is a great source of comfort and joy, it does mean that they may also be receptive to earthbound spirits. For this reason, they need to understand how to build up a strong protection around themselves.

Being too 'open'

Many of the stories included in this book have indicated how a sensitive person can pick up the emotions of an earthbound spirit and suffer fear, depression or anxiety, without even realising that the emotions they are experiencing are not their own. This applies particularly to those who are naturally mediumistic but do not understand their gift or know how to control it.

Zoe joined one of my psychic awareness groups because she wanted to understand the strange experiences she was having. Nearly every night, just as she was drifting off to sleep, she would sense earthbound spirits around her and hear them speaking to her in her head. She knew they were calling out for help but she didn't know how to help them, and she found their presence so disturbing that she couldn't sleep.

On talking to Zoe, it was clear to me that she was a natural medium. She admitted that she had had psychic experiences for as long as she could remember. She had read about earthbound spirits and regularly prayed for them. Her sympathy had attracted a number of such spirits to her and they tried to communicate with her at night because this was the time when her mind was most receptive. However, as she had not developed her mediumship she was unable to deal with them or to send them to the light.

I suggested to Zoe that the first thing she needed was to get a sound night's sleep! To enable her to do this I taught her how to 'close down' psychically so that she wouldn't be troubled by needy spirits. And I further suggested that if she felt drawn to do spirit release work, she should develop her mediumship fully so that she could use it in a controlled way.

Closing down

Closing down is something all sensitive people should do. It is a means of shutting off one's psychic awareness at times when it is not needed, in order to be centred in the physical dimension. Let me explain what I mean.

I have mentioned the aura or energy field. In addition to this, we have within the aura a number of psychic centres called chakras. The chakras are the link between the material and the spirit aspects of our being. Those most concerned in spirit communication are the solar plexus centre, situated at the navel; the heart centre; the throat centre; and the third eye centre, which is located in the forehead between and just above the physical eyes.

When mediums wish to communicate with the spirit world, they expand the aura and open the chakras, thus opening up a channel to link them with the next dimension. Mediums also know how to close down that channel at times when they are not working. Natural mediums and psychics, and people who are sensitive, tend to have an aura and chakras that are always open. They are constantly picking up impressions, not just from the spirit world but from those in this world too.

Zoe admitted that this applied very much to her. If someone around her was unhappy, she would start feeling unhappy too. If she was in the company of a person who was ill, it would not be long before she started to feel their physical symptoms. She was constantly tired and drained, another indication of being too open.

Fortunately, it is not difficult to close down. It can be done by using the following simple visualisation technique.

Exercise: Closing down

+ Sit somewhere quiet where you will not be disturbed. You may find it helpful to have some quiet music playing. Take a few deep breaths and relax.

+ Visualise a soft, warm golden light above your head. Imagine this light streaming down into the crown of your head.

+ Visualise this light descending to the third eye centre. Picture a purple-coloured flower in this centre and imagine the petals of the flower gently closing.

+ Now visualise the light descending through your head to your throat. Picture a bright blue flower at your throat centre. Imagine this flower also closing its petals.

+ Draw the light down to the heart centre. Picture a green flower here, gently closing.

+ Then draw the light down to the solar plexus centre, where there is a yellow flower which you see closing.

+ Take the light down to the base of the spine and let it travel from here, through the legs and the feet, into the ground beneath you. As you do this, imagine that you are sending roots deep down into the ground, roots that keep you firmly anchored in the physical dimension.

✦ Finally, visualise your aura as an oval of energy extending two or three feet all around your body. Imagine the golden light enveloping the whole of your aura. As you do this, feel the aura contracting a little. The light surrounds you, from head to toe. It seals you in and forms a shield.

✦ Say a prayer and send out your thoughts to the guides or loving spirits around you, to add their protection. Now you are safe and nothing harmful or negative can intrude.

When you first try this exercise you may find that it takes a little while, especially if you are not used to visualising. However, with practice you will be able to do it in a few seconds, whenever and wherever you wish.

Further means of protection

As well as using the above exercise, there are a number of other things you can do to enhance your protection:

✦ Deal with any fear you have of the supernatural. Fear is based on ignorance, so read about the subject and discuss it with those who are well informed. You might like to go to a Spiritualist church or have sittings with mediums. This will give you the reassurance that nearly all the spirits around us are kind and loving and that in the unlikely event of encountering any unpleasant spirits, you can protect yourself from harm.

✦ If you start experiencing negative emotions such as depression or anxiety that seem to have no obvious cause, try to work out where they are coming from.

These feelings could be from a spirit but it is just as likely that you are picking them up from someone living. Consider whether someone around you is suffering from such conditions.

+ If your intuition tells you that the feelings emanate from a spirit presence, you may be able to release the spirit yourself, in the way I have described. However, if you have any doubts about doing this, or feel that your attempts have not been successful and that the spirit is still there, don't hesitate to call in a medium to help you.

+ Watch your health. Sensitive people tend to be less robust than those of a more earthy nature. Have a good diet, including organic food as far as possible. Allow plenty of time for rest and relaxation. As much as you can, avoid stress. If you are tired, anxious or run down this will weaken your aura and you will be more vulnerable to the influence of earthbound spirits. (Good spirits will never harm or deplete you but will give you positive energy and healing.)

+ Avoid places where you know there has been pain and suffering in the past. A battlefields tour is not the ideal holiday for you! If you must go to such places, close down beforehand using the exercise above, and stay closed all the time you are there.

Remember that provided you are aware of the need to be vigilant and take the precautions I have listed above, you are never in any danger from the spirit world. See your sensitivity as a gift and a way of connecting with wise and loving beings who will support, guide and uphold you throughout your life.

'It's happening again!'

Some people who are natural psychics find that psychic activity follows them around wherever they go. Tony was a well-balanced, outgoing man in his twenties who had just moved into a new house with his girlfriend. They soon began to notice strange things happening. Small objects went missing then turned up again in unlikely places. After a few arguments with his girlfriend along the lines of 'Did you move my keys?' 'Don't blame me – I never touched them!' Tony concluded that some supernatural force was involved.

This wasn't the first time he had had such experiences. Similar things had occurred in his previous house. 'It's happening again!' he complained to his girlfriend, and they called me in.

While I was sitting in the house talking to Tony I saw clairvoyantly a young man who had been killed in a motorcycle accident. Tony recognised this as a friend who had died a few years before. He wanted to know whether this was the same 'ghost' that had been present in his other house, and whether it was following him around from place to place.

I told Tony I didn't think so. I explained that he was fortunate, or perhaps unfortunate, in being one of those people with a lot of psychic energy. Wherever he lived, he would be likely to attract earthbound spirits, either those already in the house or any who happened to be in the area. To these spirits, he appeared like a beacon of light. When they found that he couldn't see them they were disappointed and started using his energy to attract attention.

The spirit was helped on its way but Tony wanted to

know how he could stop this from happening again. I first showed him how to close down psychically so that he wasn't sending out such a strong signal. That way, there wouldn't be so much 'free floating' energy for any spirit to latch on to. I then suggested that, once he had thoroughly mastered the closing technique, he should consider taking up reiki or some other form of healing.

If, like Tony, you have a lot of energy, it is useless to ignore it or pretend it isn't there. Healing is an excellent way to make use of it. It is a way of channelling the energy constructively and it is also a wonderful way of helping others.

Protection at work

In Chapter 6 I described a method of cleansing your home whenever you are aware of negative energy there. But what do you do if there is negative energy, or if an earthbound spirit is present, in the place where you work?

Many years ago, I had a secretarial job in an office block in Smithfield, London. I never liked going into the building and there was not a happy working atmosphere. I was told that a couple of nightwatchmen had heard noises there at night and had been too frightened to stay. When I learned that this was the spot where many heretics had been burned at the stake in the Middle Ages, I realised why the vibrations were so unpleasant.

Clients often tell me that they are uncomfortable at work because of some presence they feel within the building. Unless you have a very understanding employer or work colleagues, you cannot go around your office or place of work burning oils and ringing bells. In cases like this, all you can do is to use prayer and visualisation, sending out thoughts and prayers for any earthbound spirit who may be trapped there. A sincere, heartfelt prayer can often reach a suffering spirit and convey the light that is able to release them.

Protecting children

Many children are psychic. They are aware of spirits around them and accept this, as I did myself, as something natural. They sometimes have 'imaginary playmates' who may in fact be spirit children. If you have a sensitive child, encourage them to talk about any psychic experiences they have. Take these experiences seriously. Don't, whatever you do, laugh at them or tell them they are imagining things. Children can very easily be made to feel foolish and hurt, and then they will be unwilling to confide in you.

They will also pick up very quickly on any fear of the supernatural you may have. Then they become fearful. Try to instil into them the idea that they have an ability that is perfectly natural but a little unusual. Warn them that they should be cautious of talking about their experiences to other children or to outsiders who may not understand, but teach them to value this ability, as it will serve them well in life.

If your child speaks of feeling a presence in the house, or seeing a ghost, listen carefully. Children are often the first to notice such things. They also, in most cases, have a natural sense of whether the spirit is friendly or nasty. I was certainly very aware, when I was growing up, of the different kinds of spirits and I would have been greatly helped if there had been anyone I could talk to about it.

Children tend to be more open psychically than adults and may need some help with closing down. If your child is old enough, you can explain the closing down exercise and perform it with them. If they are too young to understand the concept or you feel that they would be frightened by you speaking about it, then you can do it for them yourself.

Exercise: 'Closing down' a child

+ Hold the image of your child in your mind (or perhaps stand by their bed when they are asleep).

+ Visualise a golden light over your child's head. Picture this light descending through each of the psychic centres in turn (refer to the closing down exercise given earlier in this chapter).

+ Finally, visualise your child's aura extending two or three feet around the body. Now picture that golden light filling the whole aura, then wrapping it round, like a cloak. Ask your own spirit loved ones, guides, or the angels of light to keep your child safe and protected.

Healers and therapists

Many sensitive people are attracted to the caring professions and work as doctors, healers or therapists. Healers are particularly vulnerable to intrusion from earthbound spirits. When a healer is working with a client they merge and blend their aura with that of the client. As this happens, an earthbound spirit who happens to be with the client can transfer itself to the healer. Even experienced healers can be caught out in this way.

Jean was a highly qualified healer who worked at a clinic in London. When she came to see me she looked ill and was in dire need of help. 'I don't know what's wrong with me,' she complained. 'I feel as if I'm not myself any more.'

For the past few weeks she had been feeling exhausted yet unable to sleep. She was having anxiety attacks and felt guilty – yet she knew she had nothing to feel guilty about. She had been to see a couple of healers but it hadn't helped, and now she had reached the stage where she no longer felt able to continue her work.

When I tuned in, I picked up a man who had hanged himself. Jean confirmed this by saying that she often had a choking sensation for which there was no physical cause. The man was stuck because of his guilt. Having made the connection with her, he had moved with her out of the clinic into her home and now he was with her day and night.

Jean was relieved to discover the cause of her problem. We worked together to release the man and he was removed very lovingly by the guides. But she was so exhausted that she needed to close down completely and take a break from her work for a while in order to cleanse herself and restore her energy.

This was an extreme case, but all healers and therapists should be aware of their vulnerability. Even people like physiotherapists, masseurs or hairdressers who come into physical contact with members of the public, or counsellors who link with them emotionally, should take care to protect themselves.

Protection for healers and therapists

If your work brings you into contact with the public in a therapeutic context, there are a number of precautions you can take. These will protect you not just from earthbound spirits but also from any negativity emanating from your clients.

+ Before you begin your day's work, say a prayer and call upon God, the angelic forces or your own spiritual guides and helpers to give you strength and protection. Visualise your aura filled with light and see that light also filling the room where you are working.
+ Close down psychically at the end of every session. Step back from your client, either literally or in your mind, and visualise a separation between your aura and that of your client, so that the link between you is broken.
+ Pay attention to your diet and health. Take regular breaks or holidays and never allow yourself to become depleted.
+ Keep a balance in your life. Include activities that are down-to-earth rather than psychic. Keep in touch with nature by walking in the country, gardening or visiting the sea. This helps to keep you grounded.

Working from home

Many healers and therapists work from home, and they often have a room set aside for the purpose. I have my sanctuary, as I call it, which I use when I am giving sittings. I cleanse this room psychically at the beginning and end of every day. When my sitters go home, I make sure that they don't leave any earthbound spirits behind! Spirits who come from the light do not intrude uninvited, but earthbound spirits may linger – as in the case of Margaret's father, who refused to leave.

Cleansing your healing or therapy room can be as simple as visualising the room filled with white light. Crystals are helpful in absorbing negative energy so you might like to place a crystal, perhaps an amethyst, in the room. Cleanse the crystal itself regularly under running water, or by whatever method you prefer. To learn more about this subject, read some of the many books that are available on crystals and how to use them.

Remember to cleanse not just the room where you work but the whole of your home, in case some unwanted visitor has slipped past you and gone exploring the rest of the house! It is a good idea to put time aside occasionally to carry out the ritual for cleansing the house given in Chapter 6.

The greatest protection

Psychic protection is largely a matter of common sense, just as protecting yourself physically is a matter of common sense. We all know that there are murderers, muggers and other violent criminals in our society but we don't stay in our homes and refuse to go out just in case we are attacked by one. However, most people take reasonable precautions by making sure that their homes are secure and not venturing into places where they are likely to be in danger.

The same applies to psychic protection. Don't lay yourself open to the influence of earthbound spirits by using ouija boards or indulging in excessive drinking or drug taking. Don't allow yourself to become consumed with hatred or malice towards anyone, as your dark thoughts will attract dark spirits to you. Never experiment with spells or rituals designed to put a curse on anyone or to harm another person in any way. This will certainly draw dark spirits and in the end it will rebound upon you.

Try to maintain a cheerful, positive mental outlook on life, treating others with love and kindness. Develop your spiritual qualities, by prayer or meditation. Seek the light within yourself. Love, goodness and sincerity are the best and greatest protection you can have. When you send out love, you bring loving spirits to your side who will guide and guard you. If you remember these things, you will have nothing to fear.

To end this book I want to give some advice, for the benefit of those who feel that they would like to undertake spirit release, on how you can get involved in this work.

14

Doing Spirit Release Work

If you feel that you would like to do spirit release work, how do you go about it? First, obviously, you need to have mediumistic skills. Second, you need training and experience. Third, and very important, you need to be spiritually strong and to develop a positive link with your guides.

Becoming a medium

Mediums are born rather than made. You cannot decide that you would like to be a medium in the way that you can decide to learn a language or play the piano. Having said that, however, it is not such a rare gift as is generally thought. If you have ever sensed a spirit presence around you, heard a voice, either externally or in your mind, or seen a spirit, then you have mediumistic potential. How far you can develop this depends upon your innate ability and how hard you are prepared to work at it.

If you want to explore your potential, I would suggest you start by joining a Spiritualist church, so that you get a general understanding of what mediumship is all about. Read as much on the subject as you can and learn how spirits communicate with us. I have written at length on this subject in my book *Contacting the Spirit World*. You will then need to find a development circle. Many churches run such circles, which meet either in the church or in the home of the medium leading the circle.

Training to be a medium is mainly a matter of meditating and learning how to attune your mind. This is not a process that can be hurried. Some mediums sit in circles for months, some for years. It takes much effort and perseverance, patience and endless practice. When you feel ready to start using your gift for the benefit of others, you will probably be invited to take services in the church. You may also wish to give private sittings at home.

Starting spirit release work

Once you feel confident with your mediumship you will be able to decide whether you really want to undertake spirit release. As a matter of fact, you probably won't have to make this decision. I never set out to work in this way. I was drawn into it, and then discovered that it was something for which I had a vocation. All the mediums I have spoken to who perform spirit release have had the same experience. If your guides feel that you are suited to this particular task they will make this clear to you. You will, however, need some form of training.

Unfortunately, this is not easy to come by. Spirit release is not taught in most development circles as it is considered a specialised skill. Your best course is to find a medium who does such work, who will take you under their wing and allow you to work alongside them until you gain the necessary experience.

The Spirit Release Foundation

There is, however, one organisation to which you can go for training, and that is the Spirit Release Foundation (see Resources). This was set up by Dr Alan Sanderson, a highly qualified and experienced psychiatrist. Alan had become aware that some of the problems presented by his patients were due to, or aggravated by, earthbound spirits attached to them. When these spirits were released, the patients often recovered. Alan told me:

'When I learned to identify attached spirits in my patients it opened the door to a new dimension of understanding. How refreshing it was to be able to replace symptomatic treatments with one that goes to the root of the problem with a safe and gentle procedure! The discovery that the spiritual dimension has a vital influence, for good or ill, on our daily lives, was so tremendous that it had to be shared.'

In 1999, with a small group of colleagues including both psychiatrists and mediums, he set up the Foundation, its aim being to bring together all those with an interest in spirit release. Today, membership is growing rapidly, both in the UK and abroad.

Training is one of the Foundation's key activities. It offers a variety of courses ranging from the introductory to the advanced level, and covering all aspects of the subject. These courses are of value not only to mediums but to therapists and anyone working in the fields of healing or mental health. The courses require a serious commitment in terms of time and study, but for anyone who really wants to embark upon such work they give a thorough grounding. They also help students to appreciate just how deep and complex the subject is, and how important in terms of the service it provides.

Michael Evans Rescue Pack

Michael Evans, whose rescue circle in Exeter I have referred to, produces a very useful rescue pack. It includes a manual describing various techniques that have been found to be effective in rescue work, linked with two 90-minute audio tapes of actual rescues taking place. This pack contains a lot of useful information and will give you a good idea of what is involved in carrying out a rescue (see Resources).

Preparation

Spirit release is a demanding occupation. Before you embark upon it, you need to prepare yourself well. There are a number of ways in which you can do this:

+ Be well informed. Study the subject as thoroughly as you can (see the reading list at the end of this book). The more you understand about earthbound spirits, the better equipped you will be to deal with them. Also, if you have an insight into what it is like to be a spirit trapped in this condition, it will help you to reach out to such spirits with sympathy and compassion.

+ Develop mental discipline and spirituality. This alone will give you the power, the strength and the wisdom for the task you have chosen. It is your surest protection against darkness and evil.

✦ Get to know your guides. Healers and therapists, as well as mediums, have guides. When you are sitting quietly in meditation (and you should try to meditate regularly), ask these guides to make themselves known to you. Learn to recognise them, whether recognition takes the form of a name, a sensation, or just a 'knowing' that they are present. You will need to build up a strong connection with them; once this is built, you will know that you can trust them implicitly. Remember that although you are responsible for playing your part, the guides are really the ones doing the work. Do whatever is required of you with integrity and to the best of your ability, and leave the rest to them.

The importance of prayer

Do not overlook the importance of prayer. Praying regularly connects us with the highest source of love, wisdom and power. For Christians, Christ is the source of their strength, and many non-Christians respect Him as a great and holy teacher whose influence is still present in the world today. According to your own belief, you may wish to pray to Him or to another spiritual master.

You can also call upon the angels. Angels are beings of light who belong to a dimension far above anything we can conceive of, yet who reach out in loving service to this world. They are always available to help us if we seek them in sincerity and with purity of motive.

Whenever I am carrying out a rescue, I invoke both the

Christ spirit and the angels, as well as calling upon my guides. If I visit a house where there is a disturbance, I send my thoughts out constantly for strength and guidance. When the spirit has been released, before I leave I place a blessing upon the house, using the following words:

> *I call upon the Christ spirit and upon the holy angels of light to bless this house. May they fill it with their love and power. May each person here, both seen and unseen, be blessed and protected. May any spirit that is in need of help be led to a place of healing. May light and peace prevail and God's blessing be over all.*

I use a similar prayer for sitters from whom an earthbound spirit has been released:

> *I call upon the Christ spirit and the holy angels of light to bless this child of God. May (name of the sitter) be filled with love, light and healing. May he/she remain safe and protected. I call upon the Christ spirit and the holy angels of light to bless the spirit who has been released (I name the spirit, if I know the name). May he/she be taken into the light and receive peace and healing.*

When release fails

Remember that not every attempt to release an earthbound spirit will be successful. Like all mediums, I have my failures. There are a number of reasons why this may happen. Sometimes, a spirit is quite determined to stay where it is and simply refuses to budge. This is not very good for such spirits as it means that they cannot progress. If they are doing no harm, the guides will not forcibly eject them – although they will encourage them to move on as soon as they show any willingness to do so. But that may be a long time after you have left.

The most common reason, however, is that someone on earth is holding on to the spirit, perhaps because it is a loved one for whom they are grieving. It may be impossible to convince the mourner that they are hindering the spirit's progress and that letting go of it does not mean that they have to lose all contact. Understandably, they may be so absorbed in their grief that they cannot accept that this is so.

There are situations where a client finds it amusing or exciting to have a spirit around. They may say that they want it released but actually they don't, so they keep pulling it back by their thoughts. In one case I know of, an elderly widower who lived alone called in a medium because, he claimed, he was frightened of the 'evil spirit' in his house. The medium rushed over to see him, to find that in fact he wasn't frightened – he was really rather enjoying the experience. She released the spirit, who was not at all malevolent, but the following week the man called her back. He had another one.

Once again, the medium went along and released the second spirit. The next week he called again ...

It finally dawned upon her that the man was very psychic. He was also lonely and enjoying the attention she gave him. Every time she released a spirit he called in a replacement.

Just as a healer cannot cure every patient who comes to him, so a medium cannot release every spirit or help every client. Don't be too hard on yourself. There may be factors involved that you are not aware of. It may be that you are there just to start off the task and the spirit will be released later, when the time is right. You can only do your best.

Some of the most difficult cases are those where clients are suffering from some form of severe depression or mental illness. On no account attempt to deal with such cases yourself unless you have the necessary medical or psychiatric qualifications to do so. Should you be aware that there is an earthbound spirit with the client whom you can release, then of course deal with this. But refer the client to a doctor or health practitioner for further treatment.

Protection for mediums

Everything that I said in the previous chapter about protection for sensitive people, healers and therapists applies to mediums – only more so!

+ Do not overwork. Allow time for relaxation, keep a balance in your life and look after your health.
+ It is a good idea to have reiki or spiritual healing on a regular basis and to get into the habit of using self-healing techniques, preferably every day.
+ Most importantly, learn to close down when you are not working. If you do not do so you will quickly become very tired and drained.
+ If you are called out to a haunted house, arm yourself mentally with a cloak of protection before you go. Make sure that any earthbound spirits are safely despatched – don't take them home with you!
+ When working in your home, cleanse the room you use before beginning work and when you have finished.

✦ Make sure you have another medium, or perhaps a small group of people, who you can call upon if at any time you feel you need additional support. If you are uneasy about going to a haunted house, take reinforcements with you!

✦ Prayer, as I have said, is your best protection. If you work in love and sincerity, your guides will look after you and never let you down.

The need for qualified practitioners

Some mediums work exclusively in the field of spirit release. Others, like myself, carry out such work when required but concentrate mainly on giving public demonstrations of mediumship (usually called clairvoyance) in Spiritualist churches, and on offering private sittings.

I know a number of mediums who refuse to get involved in release work. Strange to say, they are afraid of getting out of their depth or coming up against forces they cannot handle. I personally believe that all mediums should have some knowledge of the subject. You cannot be a medium without sooner or later coming across earthbound spirits. It is no use pretending that they don't exist.

A lot of harm is done by inexperienced mediums and by people dabbling in spirit release who don't have the necessary skill. Not only do they fail to sort out the problem, they make matters worse by putting across their own mistaken notions and instilling fear rather than giving comfort. One client who came to me was petrified, having been told by someone who claimed to be able to release spirits that she had 61 dark entities attached to her! I don't know who counted them. As she was already in a delicate mental state, this was hardly constructive. Another client had been told by a self-styled medium that she had extra-terrestrials in her attic!

There is a great shortage of people able to carry out spirit release and unfortunately, as in every other field, charlatans are ready to prey on the vulnerable. The more mediums who qualify in this work the better. It is greatly needed, not only by earthbound spirits but also by those on earth who are suffering problems caused by such spirits.

It is also vitally important that mediums, or anyone with a knowledge of the world beyond, should do all they can to help spread that knowledge. One of the main reasons why spirits get stuck is because they are ignorant of the spiritual dimension. The more the Afterlife is understood, the better prepared people will be when the time comes for them to make that transition – and the less likely that they will become earthbound.

My prayer

One of the rewarding aspects of rescue work is that spirits who are released sometimes come back to say 'thank you'. They may then themselves join bands of rescuers and reach out to other spirits who are still in the condition from which they themselves have escaped. The task of clearing the earthly dimension of these lost souls is what spirit release is all about. Each spirit released into the light is a victory for the rescuers. And every medium who, with their guides, assists in the undertaking is strengthening the forces of light and dispelling darkness.

The New Age that we are entering is a time of enlighten-ment. My prayer is that no soul should be left behind. May all find their way to the beautiful land that is the soul's true home. My prayers also go out to all those who are seeking to help earthbound spirits. May they be given courage and wisdom to do their work well. And my thanks go to the guides and rescuers and to the holy angels, whose love and power sustains us all.

For me personally, doing spirit release has been a tremen-dous source of joy and satisfaction. I feel privileged to have been of use in this way and I am thankful to my guides who enable me to carry out this task.

I hope that this book has given you some insight into the plight of earthbound spirits and how they are released. Some of what I have said may perhaps have dismayed those who believe that everything in the spirit world is peace and happiness. But we cannot pretend that darkness and evil does not exist. We can only try to understand it, and to treat each soul with love, trusting that each one, even the darkest, may one day find the light within themselves.

If I, and all the many other mediums engaged in this work, can play just a small part in helping those who are lost and in bringing light into all the dark places of this world, then our mission will have been fulfilled.

Resources

UK

Spiritualists' National Union
Redwoods
Stansted Hall
Stansted Mountfitchet
Essex CM24 8UD
Tel 0845 4580 768
www.snu.org.uk

College of Psychic Studies
16 Queensberry Place
London SW7 2EB
Tel 020 7589 3292
www.collegeofpsychicstudies.
co.uk

*Lectures, courses, sittings,
healing, library*

Psychic News
The Coach House
Stansted Hall
Stansted Mountfitchet
Essex CM24 8UD
www.psychicnewsbookshop.co.
uk

Spiritualist newspaper

Psychic World
PO Box 14
Greenford
Middlesex UB6 OUF

Monthly Spiritualist newspaper

Spirit Release Foundation
The Administrator
Myrtles
Como Road
Malvern
Worcs WR14 2TH
Tel 07789 682420
www.spiritrelease.com

*Information on spirit release,
courses and meetings, list of
practitioners*

Michael Evans
59 The Maltings
Church Street
Exeter EX2 5EJ
www.spiritstalking.info

*Rescue pack (see Ch. 14).
£10.00 including postage &
packing*

Feng Shui Society
123 Mashiters Walk
Romford, Essex RM1 4BU
Tel 020 7050 289 200
www.fengshuisociety.org.uk

Zoence Academy
Roses Farmhouse
Epwell Road
Upper Wysoe
Warwicks CV35 OTN
Tel 01295 688185
www.zoence.co.uk

Home and environmental energetic problems, rescue work

www.spiritrescue.co.uk
Good website explaining spirit rescue

Two Words
A3 Riverside
Metropolitan Wharf
Wapping Wall
London E1W 3SS
Tel 0207 481 4332
www.users.globalnet.co.uk
Monthly spiritualist magazine

USA

National Spiritualist Association of Churches
PO Box 217, Lily Dale
NY 14752
Tel 716-595-2000
www.nsac.org

International Ghost Hunters Society
848 N. Rainbow Blvd
#592,
Las Vegas
NV 89107
www.ghostweb.com

Dave Oester & Sharon Gill. Largest internet ghost hunting society in USA

American Feng Shui Institute
111 North Atlantic Blvd
Suite 352
Monterey Park
California CA 01754
Tel. 626 571 2757
www.amfengshui.com

CANADA

International Spiritualist Alliance
1A – 320 Columbia Street
New Westminster
BC V3L 1A6
Tel 604 521 6336
www.isacanada.ca

Feng Shui Association of Canada
4841 Yonge Street
Shepherd Center
PO Box 43236
North York
Ontario M2N 6N1
www.fengshuiassociationof
canada.ca

AUSTRALIA
Aspects
PO Box 5171
Clayton
Victoria 3168
http://home.vicnet.net.au/~john
f/welcome.htm

*New Age group led by John
Fitzsimons. Information,
courses on mediumship, spirit
release, etc.*

American Spiritualist
Association
PO Box 273
Pennth
NSW 2751, Australia
Tel 1300 880 675
www.spiritualistasn.au

Bibliography and Recommended Reading

Burks, Eddie and Cribbs, Gillian, *Ghosthunter*, Headline, 1995

Crookall, Robert, *What Happens When You Die*, Colin Smythe, 1978

Denning, Hazel M., *True Hauntings*, Llewellyn, 2003

Dowding, Air Chief Marshal Lord, *Lychgate*, Rider, 1945

Evans, Michael, *Dead Rescue*, Con-Psy Publications, 2007. Available from Michael Evans, 59 The Malings, Church Street, Exeter EX2 5EJ

Furlong, David, *Working With Earth Energies*, Piatkus, 2003

Greaves, Helen, *The Wheel of Eternity*, C.W. Daniel Co., 1976

Gilbert, Alice, *Philip in Two Worlds*, Psychic Book Club, 1948

Hall, Judy, *The Crystal User's Handbook*, Godsfield, 2003

Hamilton-Parker, Craig, *What To Do When You Are Dead*, Sterling Publishing, 2001

Heathcote-James, Emma, *After-Death Communication*, Metro Publishing, 2004

Holzer, Hans, *Ghost Hunter*, Bobbs-Merrill Co. Inc., 1963

Kingston, Karen, *Creating Sacred Space With Feng Shui*, Piatkus 1996

Lawrie, Archibald A., *The Psychic Investigator's Casebook Vol. 1*, 1st Books Library, 2003 *Vol.2*, 2005, *Vol.3*, 2007. All available from Mr A.A. Lawrie, 5 Church Wynd, Kingskettle, by Cupar, Fife, Scotland KY15 7PS, UK. £14 per volume including postage and packaging, overseas $32 per volume including postage and packaging.

Linn, Denise, *Sacred Space*, Rider, 1995

Mercado, Elaine, *Grave's End*, Llewellyn, 2001

Moody, Raymond A., *Life After Life*, Rider, 1975

Muldoon, Sylvan and Carrington, Hereward, *The Projection of the Astral Body*, Rider, 1929

O'Sullivan, Terry and Natalia, *Soul Rescuers*, Thorsons, 1999

Pike, James A., *The Other Side*, W.H. Allen, 1969

Playfair, Guy Lyon, *This House is Haunted*, Souvenir, 1980

Procter, Roy and Ann, *Healing Sick Houses*, Gateway, 2000

Randall, Neville, *Life After Death*, Corgi, 1980

Williamson, Linda, *Contacting the Spirit World*, Piatkus, 1996

Williamson, Linda, *Finding the Spirit Within*, Rider, 2001

Index